TWAYNE'S WORLD AUTHORS SERIES

A Survey of the World's Literature

Sylvia E. Bowman, Indiana University

GENERAL EDITOR

DENMARK

Leif Sjöberg
State University of New York at Stony Brook

EDITOR

Meïr Goldschmidt

TWAS 414

Courtesy of The Royal Library, Copenhagen

Meïr Goldschmidt

MEÏR GOLDSCHMIDT

By KENNETH H. OBER

TWAYNE PUBLISHERS
A DIVISION OF G. K. HALL & CO., BOSTON

Library of Congress Cataloging in Publication Data

Ober, Kenneth H
      Meir Goldschmidt.

      (Twayne's world authors series ; TWAS 414 : Denmark)
      Bibliography: pp. 135–41
      Includes index.
      1. Goldschmidt, Meïr, 1819–1887.
PT8129.G5Z79   839.8'1'36 [B]   76–16525
ISBN 0–8057–6253–1

To Professor P. M. Mitchell

Contents

About the Author

Preface

Chronology

1. Meïr Goldschmidt   17

2. The Novels   61

3. Shorter Narrative Works   98

4. Dramatic Works   119

5. Goldschmidt and World Literature   125

Notes and References   131

Selected Bibliography   135

Index   143

About the Author

Kenneth H. Ober received his Ph.D. in Comparative Literature from the University of Illinois, Urbana. He has taught at Illinois State University and is the author of numerous articles and translations. His publications include contributions to *Scandinavian Studies, Slavic and East European Journal, Cornell Library Journal, Germano-Slavica, The Wordsworth Circle*, and *Orbis Litterarum* and the following translations: Meïr Goldschmidt's "Bjergtagen" in *Anthology of Danish Literature*, edited by F. J. Billeskov Jansen and P. M. Mitchell (Southern Illinois University Press, 1971) and, from Russian, M. I. Steblin-Kamenskij's *The Saga Mind* (Odense University Press, 1973). Dr. Ober, with P. M. Mitchell, also compiled the *Bibliography of Modern Icelandic Literature in Translation* (Cornell University Press, 1975).

Preface

"Goldschmidt was a little, prim person, neatly shaved, with small 'mutton-chop' whiskers, and dressed always in black. There never lived a man of letters who was more solicitous to disguise his profession in his appearance. He had been a contemporary of the romantic poets with long, wild hair, and had trampled upon their vanity with his satire. He was careful to look as much as possible like a respectable tradesman."

"Goldschmidt was a little, strongly built man, with a compact bearing and a quick gait, dark, with sharp features, with a shrewd, piercing glance, and with an exceptional faculty for communication. In conversation he was entertaining and lively. He was winning when he wanted to be, and yet there was something about him which seemed to push one back. With his life's protracted conflicts, with the consciousness of having lived for a time as one whose hand was against everybody and everybody's against him, he had become distrustful. He was constantly on his guard, always self-preoccupied, anxious about his dignity, easily wounded and easily wounding others."

Thus was the nineteenth-century Danish writer Meïr Goldschmidt described by two men—one English, one Danish—who were personally closely acquainted with him. The first was the critic and translator Sir Edmund Gosse (1849–1929), who described Goldschmidt in an obituary notice in the British journal *The Athenæum* for 27 August 1887;[1] the second was the great literary critic Georg Brandes (1842–1927), who characterized Goldschmidt also in an obituary article, reprinted in Brandes' *Samlede Skrifter* (*Collected Writings*).[2]

Goldschmidt is now little known to readers of English, although around the middle of the last century translations of several of his works were popular in England, and English translations of some of his short stories have been reprinted repeatedly and are still being published in anthologies. Indeed, Goldschmidt came close to launching himself as a novelist and short-story writer in English in London in the 1860s. He was acquainted with most of the important literary figures of his day in Scandinavia, including N. F. S. Grundtvig, Hans Christian Andersen, Henrik Ibsen, the later Nobelist Bjørnstjerne Bjørnson, and Georg Brandes. In fact, Ibsen once complained to his—and Goldschmidt's—publisher that Goldschmidt was being paid almost twice the rate Ibsen was receiving. In London Goldschmidt was acquainted with Dickens, Bulwer Lytton, Thackeray (Goldschmidt published an article in *The Cornhill Magazine*, which Thackeray edited for a time), and Disraeli, among others. He published in such well-known English journals as *Macmillan's Magazine, The Athenæum, The Victoria Magazine, Chambers's Journal*, and *Once a Week*, in addition to *The Cornhill Magazine*.

The only biographical study of Goldschmidt published prior to the 1960s was Hans Kyrre's two-volume *M. Goldschmidt*.³ Since 1960, however, a reawakening of appreciation for Goldschmidt has been taking place, as attested by Morten Borup's editions of his letters, Mogens Brøndsted's two books, Elias Bredsdorff's work on Goldschmidt's *Corsaren* period, and an increasing number of critical articles in learned journals. In 1974 the Danish radio broadcast a series on Goldschmidt, and published a selection of texts by and about Goldschmidt, edited by Jørgen Gustava Brandt: *Meïr Goldschmidt, digteren og journalisten: En mosaik af tekster (Meïr Goldschmidt, the Writer and the Journalist: A Mosaic of Texts)*. There has been no biographical or critical study of Goldschmidt in English, however.

The present study would bring this important writer to the attention of modern readers of English and attempt to make a contribution to the general revival of interest in him. Kyrre's study contains small inaccuracies (some of which are carried over from Goldschmidt's autobiography), individually trivial but collectively misleading. Subsequent scholars have tended to perpetuate them, sometimes adding small misinterpretations of their own, coupled with minor subjective judgments which are at best questionable. An example of the latter is Morten Borup's sweeping rejection of Goldschmidt's command of English, in the face of the testimony of Edmund Gosse, who knew Goldschmidt personally. The present study should help to

Preface

correct some of these troublesome and persistent inaccuracies, and cast some new light on the obscurities in his life and works. Perhaps it may encourage new English translations of those works by Goldschmidt which have lasting and universal interest.

Since practically every major event in Goldschmidt's life was assimilated into his works, it is impossible to separate his life from his works. It is also difficult to separate fiction from fact in his autobiography. His imaginative writings provide as much reliable information on Goldschmidt's life as does *Livs Erindringer og Resultater* (*Life's Recollections and Results*), which cannot be relied upon blindly, since he sometimes confused and romanticized details of his life. By the time he wrote his autobiography, he was obsessed by his "Nemesis" philosophy—he called it a religion—which denied all chance or coincidence, so that every major event in his early life was reinterpreted as being significant for a later event or condition. Goldschmidt thus unconsciously altered the causes and effects of many incidents in his life.

All his life, Goldschmidt wanted to be accepted as a Dane, but was constantly being reminded by his opponents (as was the younger critic Georg Brandes) that he was a Jew and therefore an outsider. It is, however, impossible to separate Goldschmidt the Dane from Goldschmidt the Jew in his writings, and some of Goldschmidt's finest creations are his Jewish stories and Jewish characters.

Since Goldschmidt's journalistic activities form such an important part of his development as a writer, and since his notorious—and still often misrepresented—feud with Søren Kierkegaard was carried on in his periodical *Corsaren*, this aspect of his work must be examined in some detail. Goldschmidt's political aspirations and activities, closely associated with his journalism, will be treated less thoroughly, since the Danish domestic and foreign political questions of Goldschmidt's day do not hold great interest for a non-Danish reading public.

I am indebted in more ways than I can enumerate to Professor P. M. Mitchell of the University of Illinois, who introduced me to Danish literature in general and to Goldschmidt in particular. A grant from the American Philosophical Society's Penrose Fund enabled me to work in the Royal Library, Copenhagen, where Goldschmidt's unpublished papers are preserved. I owe much to the staff of the Royal Library, as well as to that of the University of Illinois Library. Further, I must express my gratitude to the following persons individually, for invaluable help and advice generously given: Dr. Elias Bredsdorff of Cambridge University; Julius Margolinsky, Librarian, Copenhagen; Knud Wentzel, *mag. art.*, Copenhagen; David Carrington, Librarian, *The Jewish Chronicle*, London; Erla Broekema, Librarian, the Jews' College, London; and Susan Winter of the Library of the Jewish Theological Seminary of America.

KENNETH H. OBER

Chronology

1819   Meïr (originally Meyer) Goldschmidt born in Vordingborg, a town south of Copenhagen on the island of Zealand (Sjælland), on 26 October.

1825   Sent to live with orthodox relatives in Copenhagen, to attend school and to be educated in orthodox Judaism.

1827   Rejoins his parents, now in Valby, at that time a separate village (now a suburb of Copenhagen).

1829   Family moves into Copenhagen.

1833   Family moves to Næstved (another town on Zealand); Goldschmidt placed in Copenhagen's most respected school.

1836   Fails to receive the expected highest mark on university qualifying examinations.

1837   University studies at the University of Copenhagen. On 3 October he begins his first journalistic venture, the provincial weekly *Nestved Ugeblad eller Præstø Amts Tidende* (*Næstved Weekly or Præstø District News*), in 1839 changed to *Sjællandsposten eller Nestved og Callundborg Ugeblad* (*Zealand Post or Næstved and Kalundborg Weekly*).

1839   Sells the publication and is joined in Copenhagen by his mother and two sisters.

1840   The first number of Goldschmidt's satirical opposition journal *Corsaren* (*The Corsair*) appears on 8 October.

1843   Tried and eventually convicted for several articles in *Corsaren*, sentenced to "lifelong" censorship. Takes the first of many trips abroad, this time to Paris.

1845   Has an affair with Johanne Sonne, daughter of a Copenhagen ship's master, resulting in birth of a son, Adolf. Publishes first novel, *En Jøde* (*A Jew*). *Corsaren*'s feud with Søren Kierkegaard begins in December.

1846   Sells *Corsaren* in October, publishes *Fortællinger* (*Stor-*

ies). Goes abroad, visits Leipzig, Prague, Vienna, Venice, Florence, among other cities.

1847   Visits Rome and several other cities in Italy, Bern, Zürich, and returns to Copenhagen via Berlin. In December appears the first number of his new periodical *Nord og Syd* (*North and South*).

1848   A daughter, Theodora, born to Johanne Sonne. Marries Johanne; marriage dissolved in 1852.

1849   Makes his first trip to Norway, visits Andreas Munch, Jørgen Moe, Welhaven. Receives audience with King Oscar I.

1851   Makes first of many trips to England.

1853   The lengthy novel *Hjemløs* (*Homeless*) begins appearing serially in *Nord og Syd*; the final three installments published in 1857.

1854   Again in London, meets Dickens, Townshend, Bulwer Lytton, and Disraeli.

1859–   *Blandede Skrifter* (*Mixed Writings*).
1860

1861   Begins publishing a new weekly, *Hjemme og Ude* (*At Home and Abroad*); publishes *Rabbi Eliezer*. Leaves for England in August, planning to settle in England and become a writer of English; remains there until 1863.

1862   Last journalistic effort, *Norden* (*The North*).

1863   Leaves London for Rome in January; remains there until May, then returns to Copenhagen via London. Publishes *Svedenborgs Ungdom* (*Swedenborg's Youth*).

1863–   *Fortællinger og Skildringer* (*Stories and Descriptions*),
1865   containing the novel *Arvingen* (*The Heir*).

1865   *Dagbog fra en Reise paa Vestkysten af Vendsyssel og Thy* (*Journal of a Trip on the West Coast of Vendsyssel and Thy*) and *Breve fra Choleratiden* (*Letters from the Time of the Cholera*).

1867   *En Hedereise i Viborg-Egnen* (*A Trip through the Heath in the Viborg District*), *Kjærlighedshistorier fra mange Lande* (*Love Stories from many Lands*), *Ravnen* (*The Raven*), *En Roman i Breve* (*A Novel in Letters*, the second edition of *Breve fra Choleratiden*), *En Skavank* (*A Flaw*), and *Den Vægelsindede paa Graahede* (*The Fickle Girl on Graahede*).

1868– *Smaa Fortællinger* (*Little Stories*).
1869

1869 *Rabbi'en og Ridderen* (*The Rabbi and the Knight*), a reworking of *Rabbi Eliezer*; *I den anden Verden* (*In the Other World*).

1871 *Avrohmche Nattergal.*

1877 *Livs Erindringer og Resultater* (*Life's Recollections and Results*) (Volume 2 contains *Nemesis*); and *Fortællinger og Virkelighedsbilleder, ældre og nye,* (*Stories and Pictures of Reality, older and new*).

1883 *Fortællinger og Virkelighedsbilleder: Ny Samling* (*Stories and Pictures of Reality: New Collection*).

1887 Goldschmidt dies on 15 August in Copenhagen and is buried in Copenhagen's Vestre Jewish Cemetery. *Smaa Skildringer fra Fantasi og fra Virkelighed* (*Little Descriptions from Fantasy and from Reality*) published by Goldschmidt's son.

CHAPTER 1

Meïr Goldschmidt

I "I am of the Tribe of Levi"

WITH the words, "I am of the Tribe of Levi," Goldschmidt began the story of his life, *Livs Erindringer og Resultater* (*Life's Recollections and Results*). This meant that traditionally in certain ceremonies in the synagogue, the presumed descendants of this caste of temple officials took precedence over all other Jews except descendants of the *cohanim*, the highest caste of priests. The Goldschmidt family's claim to this honor was presumably based on their name, as referring to the Levites' duties of caring for the temple treasures. Goldschmidt himself traced his lifelong ambition to be first, in whatever activity he undertook, back to the consciousness of belonging to this elite. As is the case with much in Goldschmidt's autobiographical writings, this statement must not be taken too literally, but it does present an interesting sidelight on Goldschmidt's aristocratic psychology and helps to explain the agonizing wounds constantly inflicted on his pride throughout his life, primarily by his gentile opponents.

Goldschmidt's father's family had come to Copenhagen from Hamburg in the early eighteenth century, and his maternal grandfather had immigrated to Denmark from a small town on the German-Polish border, and had settled in the provincial town of Roskilde. As a result of the order of 1814 requiring permanent last names, he, like many other Jews, took a place-name as a family name—Roskilde, which was given the German form Rothschild. Thus by coincidence, one branch of Goldschmidt's relatives came to share a name which later became synonymous with great wealth. To add to the coincidence, Goldschmidt's

cousin Benjamin Rothschild, who settled in London, became
a millionaire himself through the diamond trade.

After his marriage in 1819, Goldschmidt's father Aron established himself as a merchant in Vordingborg. This was the year
that the anti-Jewish riots and persecutions spread to Denmark
from Hamburg. Aron took his pregnant wife to the nearby home
of his brother-in-law when the mobs gathered to plunder the
Jews' homes and businesses. There the Jewish men armed themselves with axes and waited. At the last moment, the town's
three police officials managed to disperse the mob without
further violence, but Goldschmidt's parents never forgot the
terror of that day. Soon afterward Meyer was born. His mother's
descriptions of the terrifying incident made a deep impression
on the boy, for Goldschmidt later described it in both his first
novel *En Jøde* (*A Jew*) and his autobiography.

There were not enough Jews in Vordingborg to support a
synagogue or organized Jewish community life, and Goldschmidt's parents did not observe orthodox ceremonies, and did
not live kosher. As a boy, he was not exposed to much overt
prejudice or persecution, partly thanks to the protection of
his cousins, who had inherited their father's unusual size and
strength. Until he was seven years old, he had little knowledge
of Jewish ceremonial life.

In his autobiography Goldschmidt attributed an almost mystical significance to the fact that his mother sang to him in
Danish rather than Yiddish. He saw in this a refutation of the
assertion by N. F. S. Grundtvig (1783–1872) that the Danish
language and culture were actually foreign to him. In view of
the fact that the Jewish-born writer Henrik Hertz (1798–1870)
also emphasized the influence exerted on his writing by the
Danish folk songs which his mother had sung to him, Goldschmidt may have been exaggerating or romanticizing. In any
event, Goldschmidt's mother, who lived with him and his sister
Ragnhild from 1839 until her death in 1870, always exercised
a strong influence over him.

When Goldschmidt was six years old, his father decided to
take him to Copenhagen so that the boy might attend a better
school. He was to live with Aron's sister and her husband
Heyman Levin, who maintained a strict orthodox home. It was

the intention of Goldschmidt's father that the boy should now make up for his almost complete lack of orthodox Jewish training. During the year he spent with his uncle, Goldschmidt was thoroughly exposed to Jewish ritual life, both in the home and in the synagogue, but it was especially the ceremonies conducted in the home, with the uncle presiding, which made a permanent impression on the boy. It was during this period, too, that Goldschmidt became acutely aware of anti-Semitism in Danish society. Like virtually all the major impressions received by Goldschmidt, these were later to be made use of in his novels and short stories.

While Goldschmidt was absorbing orthodoxy in his uncle's home in Copenhagen, his father had been forced to give up his business in Vordingborg, and had bought a farm in Valby, in the twentieth century a suburb of Copenhagen, but at that time a separate village. After rejoining his parents there, Goldschmidt lived three years in these rural surroundings, while attending school in Copenhagen. In 1829 his father had once again to give up their home, and the family moved into Copenhagen, where Aron bought a share in a trading ship carrying grain to England. But Aron's bad luck continued, and the ship was lost. The English insurance agent embezzled the insurance payment, and the elder Goldschmidt was never able to recover the money. (As an example of Goldschmidt's abnormal preoccupation with his "Nemesis" idea—the divine order or justice—in later life, he lent great significance to the fact that he received the exact amount of the lost insurance payment, in the form of author's fees, from England.)

In 1833, the Goldschmidt family moved to Næstved, a town in southern Zealand, but Goldschmidt was placed in von Westen's Institute, which had the reputation of being the best preparatory school in Copenhagen. He lived with a relative of his mother's, who did not observe strict orthodoxy. The director of the school, Vilhelm August Borgen (1801–1884), greatly impressed Goldschmidt as a tolerant, enlightened humanist. During the three years Goldschmidt spent at the school—for the most part, a happy time for him—he was usually at the top of his class. He and another boy vied for the highest honors, but the other boy usually won, on at least one occasion unjustly.

Interestingly, one of Goldschmidt's favorite classes at the school was fencing. He seems to have become an expert, and in his autobiography he tells of two occasions in 1847 in Italy when possession of a sword cane and the knowledge of its use possibly saved his life.

Goldschmidt expected to pass the final examinations, which would qualify him for entering the university, with the highest honors. But when he took the examinations, in 1836, a low mark on one of the examinations—religion (that is, Christianity)—brought his overall mark too low to qualify him for these honors. This was apparently one of the greatest disappointments of his life, and it was a devastating blow to his father. The latter had cherished vague hopes of his son's becoming a great rabbi or a great doctor, and the first step toward either career was to have been highest honors on the examinations. Goldschmidt entered the university, but the glamor had gone from student life. True to his habit of seeing symbols everywhere when he looked back on his life, he later remembered that on his way to take the examinations, he had suddenly noticed the shadow of the great church near the university falling across his path like an obstacle.

Many of his experiences at the school are reflected in Goldschmidt's works, especially the novel En Jøde (A Jew). During the years he spent at von Westen's Institute, he became almost Christianized, although he was never baptized. The influence of his orthodox uncle's home was almost totally eclipsed by that of Borgen.

During his first year at the university, Goldschmidt fell in love. He does not reveal the name of the girl in his autobiographical writings, and the infatuation did not last long. The experience was, however, important for two reasons. It was the first adult manifestation of the strongly erotic side of Goldschmidt's nature, which was to cause Goldschmidt to fall frequently in love, often with married women. It was also the first of many times when Goldschmidt was to sublimate his feelings in literature. This time it resulted, apparently, in a short story, which he offered to the publisher A. P. Liunge (1798–1879). Liunge, however, emphatically rejected it as "trash." Goldschmidt's first venture as a writer had not been promising.

II *Journalistic Debut*

At this time, Goldschmidt was receiving assistance from an uncle in Kalundborg, a town on the west coast of Zealand. On a vacation visit to this uncle, Goldschmidt became involved in a disagreement with him, and the uncle reminded him of his failure to receive highest honors on his examinations. Furious, Goldschmidt left his uncle's house and walked all the way back to Copenhagen—the trip took him twenty-one hours—to rejoin his father. He then returned to Næstved with his father to try to hit upon some way to replace his uncle as a source of support. He wanted to publish his stories, and it occurred to him that he had seen a new weekly which had begun publication in Kalundborg, and he resolved to start a provincial periodical himself. If his stories were not good enough for Copenhagen, perhaps they would meet with a better reception in the provinces. The result was the *Nestved Ugeblad eller Præstø Amts Tidende* (*Næstved Weekly or Præstø District News*). The first issue appeared on 3 October 1837, and Goldschmidt's long, distinguished career as a journalist and imaginative writer was launched. He was at this time not yet eighteen years old.

Since there was no suitable printer in the district, Goldschmidt had his weekly printed in Copenhagen—a convenient arrangement since he was continuing his studies at the university. He soon personally visited his subscribers, however, for one of them had written him an anonymous letter asking for fewer of his short stories and more material of local interest, and Goldschmidt complied by visiting and talking to his readers in person. He soon became interested in local political questions, and his weekly reflected this interest.

Censorship was such at the time in Denmark that the periodicals which were authorized to carry foreign news also were subjected to preprinting and secret censorship control, while those entitled to carry only domestic news—and these were largely provincial periodicals—were reviewed by the censors only after printing, and if an article was objected to, that number of the publication was confiscated and a public court process might follow. The censorship officials were therefore inclined to avoid publicity and permit articles to be printed in the provincial papers which would not have passed the censor in the capital. The provincial press took on an importance that it otherwise would not have had, and the public read these provincial publications carefully, hoping to find the type of political news which never appeared in the major periodicals of the capital.

In January 1839 the *Nestved Ugeblad* was merged with the *Callundborg Ugeblad* (*Kalundborg Weekly*) and renamed *Sjællandsposten eller Nestved- og Callundborg-Ugeblad* (*The Zealand Post or Næstved and Kalundborg Weekly*), and appeared twice weekly. This periodical ran until the end of 1839, and by this time Goldschmidt, who had started his journalistic venture as a vehicle for his own literary efforts, had become known, in a modest way, as a liberal and progressive editor. But he had also had his first brush with the censor, who brought charges against him. The court process dragged on, and eventually ended with Goldschmidt being fined and sentenced to one year's personal censorship. Before the court case was finally decided, however, Goldschmidt had sold his paper for a handsome sum. His family had divided—his father and a younger brother had gone to Falster to establish a small factory—and Goldschmidt found himself the sole means of support of his mother and two sisters in Copenhagen. He worked for a short time for the conservative Copenhagen newspaper *Dagen*, and then embarked upon the most misunderstood and misrepresented period of his life, one which resulted in misconceptions that have been perpetuated to the present day. He conceived the idea of the satirical opposition periodical *Corsaren* (*The Corsair*), and kept it going for six years, largely singlehanded.

III   Corsaren

The old king, Frederik VI (1768–1839; reigned 1808–1839), had just died, and the new king, Christian VIII (1786–1848; reigned 1839–1848), soon disappointed high hopes for a more liberal government. The demand for a liberal constitution and freedom of the press was beginning to make itself heard. Attending a newly founded liberal association, "Akademisk Læseforening" ("Academic Reading Union"), Goldschmidt discussed the new liberal demands, and the need for a satirical weekly publication in opposition to the conservatives was brought up, apparently by Poul Chievitz (1817–1854). (Chievitz became a minor writer of novels, stories, and plays.) Goldschmidt, who had just sold his periodical and thus had a little capital, offered to finance the project, and another young man of the group suggested the name *Corsaren,* after the French satirical publication *Le Corsaire-Satan.* Goldschmidt set up a figurehead editor, and since the others soon withdrew from the project, it was Goldschmidt who wrote most of the material published in the periodical until 1846, when he sold it.

From the first number, which came out on 8 October 1840, the avowed program of *Corsaren* was to avoid the positions of both the conservatives and the radicals, and to steer a middle course but to work for the abolition of the absolute monarchy. The periodical soon had three thousand subscribers, an extraordinary number for the time. The caricatures (previously unknown in Danish periodicals) and the regular column "Charivari," a collection of witty and satirical stories on the French model, made *Corsaren* popular with all levels of readers—even the king was said to read it regularly. The satirical element overshadowed the serious side of the journal—the articles on literature, for example, which Goldschmidt had intended to publish in order to help maintain standards in literature and the theater were crowded out. Because of this critical, negative, and satirical character of *Corsaren* Goldschmidt acquired the undeserved reputation for vicious, malicious character assassination that has endured to the present.

Corsaren was predictably plagued by official confiscations and court processes (since it was not privileged to carry articles on foreign affairs, it was not subjected to secret preprinting censorship), but Goldschmidt's succession of shadow editors apparently delayed his being brought into court himself. Inevitably, the confiscations resulted in widened circles of readers. Once Goldschmidt slyly turned the confiscations to his advantage—a number of *Corsaren* appeared with blank pages, except for a drawing of a little man with a big nose. The public interpreted this as a symbol of the government censor and confiscation, but the actual fact was that Goldschmidt had been taken up with holiday social affairs to the extent that he simply had not had time to prepare the manuscript for that number.

In 1842, Goldschmidt's literary development took a new direction, and the stimulus for this change literally came knocking on his door, in the person of Peder Ludvig Møller. Møller (1814-1865) was a talented literary critic and Casanova-like character who had just returned from a visit to the Norwegian poet Henrik Wergeland (1808–1845). The latter had sent his greetings, along with a pouch of tobacco, to Goldschmidt. From Norway Møller also brought the message that *Corsaren* was so good that it deserved to be a Norwegian journal!

Møller twice won Copenhagen University's gold medal for essays, once for a treatment of French poetry and again for a literary historical work on the comedy in France and Denmark. He avowedly intended to change the course of Danish literary criticism. At the time he met Goldschmidt, he had already published critical articles in periodicals, and himself later published the periodical *Arena* and the annual *Gæa*. He wanted to be named Oehlenschläger's successor as professor of aesthetics in the university. He was thus Goldschmidt's superior in matters of artistic taste and appreciation, and he virtually educated Goldschmidt in aesthetics. Theirs was apparently an unusual friendship, for although they were associated for years, they never addressed each other with the familiar pronoun "du," and Møller never abandoned his superior, at times sarcastic, manner with Goldschmidt. Goldschmidt later portrayed Møller in his novel *Hjemløs* (*Homeless*).

It was no longer a secret that Goldschmidt alone was the editor of *Corsaren,* and a court process against him for some of the confiscated material was instituted. A lower court acquitted him, but the verdict was appealed to a higher court. In the meantime, although Goldschmidt was critical of the Scandinavian union movement among the students, when a Scandinavian students' trip to Uppsala was organized in June 1843, he was invited to participate by one of the movement's leaders, the writer and politician Carl Ploug (1813–1894). Goldschmidt, who had always been made to feel the outsider because he was a Jew, was flattered and touched, and agreed to go along. On the return trip, when the students' ship landed at Malmö to disembark Swedish students, Goldschmidt saw Møller waiting at the dock. Møller brought the news that the higher court had overturned Goldschmidt's acquittal, and that he had been sentenced to a total of twenty-four days (six periods of four days each) at "bread and water." Even though this sentence is not to be taken too literally, the news came as a shock to Goldschmidt. An additional sentence imposed "lifelong" personal censorship on him.

Møller defended Goldschmidt in his publication *Arena*, and when Goldschmidt decided, on completion of his sentence, to go to Paris to "see, forget, learn, enjoy, grow" as he wrote in his autobiography, Møller took over the job of editing *Corsaren*.

This was the first of Goldschmidt's many trips abroad. He became part of the tradition of much-traveled Danish writers, such as Ludvig Holberg, Jens Baggesen, and Hans Christian Andersen, and his impressions and experiences were extensively reflected in his first three novels. This first trip lasted only a short time, and in November 1843, he was back in Copenhagen. That he not only "learned," but "enjoyed" is attested by a letter he wrote to Møller from Paris telling of his conquest of a Parisian grisette.[1]

Møller, whose own love affairs kept gossips busy, was probably instrumental in bringing Goldschmidt together with Johanne Marie Sonne (1825–1900), the daughter of a Christianshavn ship's master. Their liaison lasted for several years, beginning in the early 1840s, and resulted in 1845 in the birth of a son, Adolf (1845–1912), whom Goldschmidt raised, and a daughter, Theodora (1848–1914), who remained with her mother. Goldschmidt reportedly doubted that the girl was his daughter. In order to legitimize the son, the parents entered into a *pro forma* marriage in 1848; the marriage was annulled in 1852, and the couple never actually lived together.

Although the sentence of lifelong censorship prevented Goldschmidt from openly resuming the editorship of *Corsaren*, he could still appear as its "publisher," and continued in actual fact to write most of the material which appeared in it. He could also resume his political activity, and on 4 July 1844 he attended a mass meeting on the Schleswig-Holstein question at Skamlingsbanke in Jutland, where he, along with Grundtvig and others, made a public speech. The speech is important, possibly, only because his opening words have become almost a commonplace since they have been used—by Goldschmidt himself and by practically all who have written about him—as a kind of slogan to typify Goldschmidt's strivings both as a political activist and as a writer: "I am a Jew; what do I want among you?" ("Jeg er en Jøde, hvad vil jeg imellem Jer?").

It was at this meeting, too, that Goldschmidt met the first of a series of women with whom he entertained the idea of marriage—one of love and understanding, in contrast to his relationship with Johanne Sonne. After his speech, the woman, Pauline Seidelin, approached him, and they soon opened their hearts to each other. Goldschmidt went home with her, and after his return to Copenhagen they corresponded ardently for a time. Setting a pattern for Goldschmidt's future sudden infatuations, however, the relationship cooled and Goldschmidt returned to Johanne.

According to Goldschmidt, it was Møller who gave him the idea for writing his first novel, A Jew. As with all such statements on Goldschmidt's part neatly pinpointing one cause and one effect—and it was characteristic of his later obsession with his Nemesis philosophy that he constantly sought or invented such one-to-one relationships in looking back over his life—this assertion should perhaps not be accepted unconditionally. Møller probably was the immediate impetus, however. In his memoirs Goldschmidt tells that once, in a frank conversation with Møller, he unburdened himself of all his sorrow, resentment, and bitterness over the oppressed condition of Jews, even in the relatively tolerant Denmark of the time. Evidently Møller had simply not been conscious of all the restrictions placed on Jews, and Goldschmidt quotes him as saying, as they were parting, "With feelings like those, one writes a novel." Goldschmidt remarks that he wrote the first draft of the concluding chapter of A Jew that same night.

When A Jew was published in 1845 (because of the sentence of censorship, under the name "Adolph Meyer"), it became something of a sensation. It depicts the life of a cultured and enlightened Jew from birth to death, largely in the ostensibly tolerant Denmark of Goldschmidt's own day. While there is danger in reading too much autobiography into the novel, it is woven around many of Goldschmidt's own experiences, and the bitterness which permeates the narrative is Goldschmidt's own. The novel pointed to several new directions in Danish literature. As Mogens Brøndsted, a Danish scholar, has pointed out, it was "the first Danish novel of significance which consciously has a fate develop according to the germ established in the earliest childhood years."[2] The European reading public was accustomed to the Byronic hero, pursuing some shadowy "Ideal," but being presented with such a hero who happened also to be a Jew was a new experience. Previously, Jews in Danish literature had been either comic figures, as in Holberg, or idealized, as in Blicher. Now the Jewish character was being portrayed realistically, from the inside, and it was the first time that Danish readers had been allowed an intimate, realistic look at Jewish household ceremony and synagogue ritual. This "exposé" was resented by many of the Jews of Copenhagen; mindful of recent (1819) organized anti-Jewish riots and pogroms across Europe, most of the Jewish population would have preferred to remain inconspicuous and unnoticed. Probably expressing their thought, the Danish critic Georg Brandes (1842–1927), himself of Jewish background, wrote in 1869, "Goldschmidt should not, as I once heard a witty Jew express it, constantly serve up his grandmother with sharp sauce."[3]

A Jew soon established "Adolph Meyer" not only in Denmark, where a second edition appeared in 1852 (a third came out in 1899), but abroad as well. Two different English translations appeared in 1852, one of which was reprinted in 1864; a German translation was published in 1856. (Translations have also appeared in Yiddish and Russian.)

IV Søren Kierkegaard

The year 1845, besides witnessing the appearance of Goldschmidt's first novel, was of crucial importance for his career in that it brought the beginning of Goldschmidt's notorious feud with the Danish philosopher and theologian Søren Kierkegaard. The course of the feud and its causes and effects have been distorted and misrepresented, sometimes outrageously, by

Kierkegaard scholars. Largely as a result of depending on Kierkegaard's own later descriptions of the clash, these scholars have made Kierkegaard into the innocent martyr of a vicious and unprincipled Goldschmidt. Although Elias Bredsdorff in his carefully documented book *Goldschmidts "Corsaren"* has presented the facts of the matter, some present-day Kierkegaard researchers seem to have remained innocent of them. In actuality, the weight of blame for unethical conduct lay with Kierkegaard, and if there was a victory in the affair, it was won by Goldschmidt, who, at least at first, only responded to Kierkegaard's attacks. The real martyr in the conflict was P. L. Møller, whose career was ruined by it.

According to his memoirs, Goldschmidt first met Kierkegaard in 1837. Bredsdorff points out that Goldschmidt's memory for dates here, as elsewhere, is at fault, however—the meeting actually must have taken place late in 1838. They did not meet again until late in 1841, after a review of Kierkegaard's dissertation, *Om Begrebet Ironi med stadigt Hensyn til Sokrates* (*On the Concept of Irony, with Constant Regard for Socrates*), appeared in *Corsaren*. The two met by chance on the street, and Kierkegaard, who, like everybody else, knew that Goldschmidt was the real editor of *Corsaren*, mentioned the review, with which he was generally satisfied, and added that it lacked "comic composition," on which Goldschmidt should concentrate. Goldschmidt apparently did not understand what Kierkegaard had in mind, but they parted quite cordially, and they subsequently met and conversed frequently on the streets of Copenhagen. In February 1843, Kierkegaard published his *Enten-Eller* (*Either-Or*) under the name "Victor Eremita" and Goldschmidt, deeply impressed by the book, reviewed it in *Corsaren*.

Goldschmidt's *A Jew* appeared in November 1845, and was reviewed in the popular weekly *Fædrelandet* (*The Fatherland*). Kierkegaard and Goldschmidt met on the street soon after, and Kierkegaard, discussing the review, which had been largely favorable, interpreted it as signifying that the critics wished to see in Goldschmidt the author of the successful novel, rather than the editor of the suspect periodical *Corsaren*. Kierkegaard added that *Corsaren* was identified with P. L. Møller. Shocked, Goldschmidt tried to convince Kierkegaard that he, Goldschmidt, was sole editor of the periodical; he knew that Møller, who had contributed only a very few articles, did not want to publicize too much his connection with *Corsaren* since he still hoped to be named professor of aesthetics at the university—an appointment which would be jeopardized if he were labeled as permanent editor of *Corsaren*. Kierkegaard, who detested Møller, continued to insist that the latter was the spirit behind *Corsaren*.

In view of his low opinion of Møller and of *Corsaren* in general, Kierkegaard was not overly flattered when he was praised in an article in the periodical later the same year. The final upheaval came, however, as a result of an article, not in *Corsaren,* but in Møller's literary annual *Gæa,* which came out around Christmas. Kierkegaard's *Stadier paa Livets Vei* (*Stages on Life's Way*) had appeared in April, but it was not reviewed until Møller's article appeared. Møller's review had some praise for Kierkegaard, and the article was generally perceptive and astute, but it contained personal slurs as well. Kierkegaard responded with an explosive article in *Fædrelandet* personally attacking Møller and exaggerating his connection with *Corsaren*. Kierkegaard demanded to be criticized in *Corsaren* in the same way as other noted figures were. He did not want to be the only Danish writer to be praised in the journal, he said. To Møller and Goldschmidt, this was a gross violation of the rules—one simply did not turn literary criticism, no matter how sharp, into an excuse for a violent, uncalled-for personal attack in the periodical press. Møller responded briefly in print to this effect, but the damage had already been done to his hopes for a professorship and to his position as a leading literary critic. He soon abandoned all hope of a career in Denmark and went abroad. He never returned to Denmark, but died ill and impoverished in France.

Goldschmidt took up the challenge, however—and this Kierkegaard evidently had not expected. Fighting back for both his friend and his periodical, Goldschmidt published, on 2 January 1846, a comic article in *Corsaren* ridiculing Kierkegaard (without mentioning his name, but playing upon Kierkegaard's many pseudonyms) and *Fædrelandet*. In the next number, of 9 January, *Corsaren*'s first caricature of Kierkegaard appeared—a crude but effective effort by *Corsaren*'s caricaturist Peter Klæstrup (1820–

1882). As Bredsdorff points out, the drawing has become a classic. It ridiculed Kirkegaard's posture, his exaggerated style of tailoring, and—true or not—his trousers with one leg shorter than the other. Although Kierkegaard had provoked the counterattack and perhaps deserved the satire in Goldschmidt's articles, this caricature and others to follow seemed cruel. *Corsaren* soon made Kierkegaard a laughingstock on the streets of Copenhagen.

Kierkegaard responded in *Fædrelandet,* and *Corsaren* continued to ridicule Kierkegaard throughout the summer of 1846, but the level of taste in the "wit" of the articles was not particularly high. Kierkegaard's notes and diary entries show how deeply the attacks in *Corsaren* affected him. They became an obsession with him, and he lost sight of the real situation, and frequently falsified the true causes and effects of the feud. He thought of himself as an innocent martyr, and subsequent scholarship has all too often accepted his fantasies as truth, and has overlooked the fact that Kierkegaard, like almost all Goldschmidt's other opponents, in the end resorted to the shabbiest of expedients—he attacked Goldschmidt simply because he was a Jew.

In retrospect, Goldschmidt also distorted the truth of the effects of the feud. In his memoirs, he wrote that the war with Kierkegaard, and the fact that the latter once met him on the street and went by without speaking, and only gave him an embittered look, so affected Goldschmidt that he immediately decided to sell *Corsaren.* In actual fact, Goldschmidt had grown tired of the constant pressures and quarrels, and of the repeated official confiscations and troubles with the censor. His success with *A Jew* had showed him that he could write imaginative literature as well as journalistic contributions. In 1846 his book of *Fortællinger* (*Stories*) was published, again over the name of "Adolph Meyer." In October 1846 he sold *Corsaren,* which continued publication until 1855, but with nothing like its success under Goldschmidt's editorship.

Another reason, and perhaps the most impelling one, for selling *Corsaren* was that Goldschmidt wanted to go abroad again, and with the proceeds from the sale of the periodical, he could now afford an extended trip through Europe.

V *The Grand Tour*

Goldschmidt's second educational and recreational trip abroad, which was to last approximately a year, would provide a rich source of inspiration and material for both his journalistic and his literary work for some time to come. It began in Hamburg, where Goldschmidt saw his brother Moritz, who had a small factory in nearby Pinneberg. His main interest, however, was in finding a German publisher for his novel and his volume of stories. He had reached an agreement with a publisher, but when Goldschmidt emphatically defended the Danish stand in the Schleswig question, the contract was withdrawn.

From Hamburg, Goldschmidt went to Leipzig, where he met the Danish composer Niels Gade (1817–1890), the Swedish-Jewish musician Jacob A. Josephson (1818–1880), the German authors Karl Gutzkow (1811–1878) and Georg Köberle (1819–1898), and a number of political radicals, including Arnold Ruge (1802–1880) and Robert Blum (1807–1848). Ruge published translations of one of Goldschmidt's articles from *Corsaren* and two stories from *Stories* in his *Taschenbuch* in 1847. Goldschmidt also managed to have a selection of articles from *Corsaren* dealing with the Schleswig-Holstein question published in German.

After short visits to Dresden and Prague, Goldschmidt proceeded to Vienna, where he met, among others, the writers Ignaz von Castelli (1781–1862), Ludwig A. Frankl (1810–1894), Leopold Kompert (1822–1886), Franz Grillparzer (1791–1872), Friedrich Hebbel (1813–1863)—whom he had met in Paris on his first trip abroad—Moritz Saphir (1795–1858), and Eduard von Bauernfeld (1802–1890).

In December, Goldschmidt left Vienna for Italy, and after a short stay in Venice, he arrived in Rome on 5 January 1847. Rome, more than any other locality, provided Goldschmidt with ideas, material, and inspiration for his writing, both journalistic and imaginative. This first stay, which lasted until April, laid the foundation for the 1863 visit, which was even more important for Goldschmidt's literary production. In 1847 Goldschmidt was at first disappointed with Rome, but this was his usual reaction to a city which he was visiting for the first time; the city he had just left always seemed almost a lost paradise. Rome overwhelmed him, and he was on the point of going on to Paris, which appealed to his journalistic instincts. But he decided to remain, and embarked upon a reading program to refresh his schoolboy knowledge of the classical writers, in order better to appreciate the monuments of art surrounding him. On the way to Rome he had met Federigo Pescantini (1802–1875), a radical political figure returning to Rome from exile, as well as the Norwegian poet Andreas Munch (1811–1884) and his wife Charlotte (1824–1850). Although Goldschmidt associated with many members of the foreign colony of Rome, the Munchs, and especially Charlotte, came to mean the most to him. Judging from Goldschmidt's writings and correspondence, he spent most of his time in Rome in the company of foreign artists and writers, but this impression is probably misleading, for he must have associated extensively with Italians. He learned the language so well that he later acted as interpreter for other foreigners in Rome, especially his "English" cousin Benjamin Rothschild.

As usual, Goldschmidt was not allowed to forget his divided nature, even in Rome. Although he was fascinated by the Catholic church in Rome, attended mass, and was captivated by the singing of the nuns in the convents, he was also drawn to the ghetto, where he was shaken by the indignities and persecutions heaped upon the Jews there.

During carnival time, Goldschmidt took part in the festivities, went to masquerade balls, and apparently had some amorous adventures. He also became infatuated with Charlotte Munch—one of the series of Goldschmidt's ambiguous relationships with married women. (It is unknown how many of Goldschmidt's infatuations involved actual seduction.)

Goldschmidt had conceived a vague idea for a novel dealing with Queen Christina of Sweden, who had converted to Catholicism; he gave this idea up, but later used the great quantity of impressions and observations he amassed in Rome for the monumental novel *Hjemløs* (*Homeless*). By now he was so enchanted by Rome that it was difficult for him to tear himself away from the city, but in April 1847 he left Rome for southern Italy. He traveled via Naples to Sicily, where he toured with the German scholar Karl Johan Tycho Mommsen (1819–1900)[4] and the German philologist Martin Hertz (1818–1895). On 2 May he reached the southern coast of Sicily, from where he could see the African coast. He soon returned to Rome, but only to take leave of his friends there, and in early June he was on his way to Switzerland, via Pisa and Genoa.

Switzerland was at the time undergoing a civil war between conservative Catholic cantons and liberal Protestant cantons— strife from which the country was to emerge a unified, free federation. Goldschmidt was struck by the fact that the Swiss hardly seemed to notice that they had three national languages, and that this in no way interfered with carrying on the business of governmental administration. He compared this with the situation in Schleswig-Holstein, which at that time was still under Danish rule, and in which the language difference was the source of bitter conflict. Swiss ideas of freedom, democracy, and multilingualism so impressed Goldschmidt that he decided to bring home to the Danish people what he had learned, perhaps through a new periodical, perhaps through a novel.

In Geneva, Bern, and Zürich Goldschmidt met many of the Swiss political leaders. More important for his own development were his talks with a Protestant clergyman named Piguet, whose humanistic Christianity made a more lasting impression on Goldschmidt's thinking than had his flirtation with Catholicism.

In August Goldschmidt returned to Germany, after having visited Lausanne, Lucerne, Schwyz, and Einsiedeln. He returned to Leipzig, but his overwhelming experiences since his first visit dulled the city's glamor somewhat. The last stop on his return trip was Berlin, where he met Karl A. Varnhagen von Ense (1785–1858), who with his Jewish wife Rahel (1771–1833) had held a salon for the "Junges Deutschland" literary group. Varnhagen von Ense gave Goldschmidt a letter of introduction to Heinrich Heine which Goldschmidt was to use in Paris in 1850. Goldschmidt was once more in Copenhagen in October 1847.

VI Nord og Syd

Goldschmidt immediately set to work carrying out a plan to establish a new political, social, and economic periodical

which would bring to the Danish public the political lessons
he had learned during his year abroad, especially in Switzerland.
The new venture bore the name *Nord og Syd* (*North and
South*), which symbolized Goldschmidt's sources for his pro-
posals for the solutions of Denmark's political problems. Goldschmidt supported the maintenance of a constitutional federa-
tive government which would include Holstein as well as
Schleswig, an idea which would be rejected by Denmark's
political leaders, ultimately with disastrous results for Denmark.

In contrast to *Corsaren, Nord og Syd* was not satirical or
witty, but was a serious, mature journal, not the least important
contributions to which were Goldschmidt's theatrical and critical
articles. What he perhaps lacked in profound literary critical
instinct, he made up for in enthusiasm and interest. Like
Corsaren, Nord og Syd was made up almost entirely of Goldschmidt's own contributions. At first it appeared monthly, and
since Goldschmidt was still under "lifelong" censorship (the
sentence was lifted by the general amnesty of the new king,
Frederik VII [1808–1863; reigned 1848–1863], after the death
of Christian VIII on 20 January 1848), he could not at first
identify himself as editor. The journal did not cease publication
until 1859.

Goldschmidt's hopes for exercising political influence (as a
Jew, he could have no hope of ever being an elected official)
were shattered time after time, although he almost always had
the bitter satisfaction of seeing himself proved right when it was
too late. When he attempted to point out the dangers of the
prevalent nationalistic, overly patriotic attitudes of the political
leaders, he was accused, notably by the religious thinker and
writer N. F. S. Grundtvig (1783–1872), of not being a true
Dane, but only a guest in Denmark—one who had no right to
criticize anything Danish or to suggest to the Danes that they
were not following the correct path. This was the same line
of attack pursued by almost all of Goldschmidt's adversaries
sooner or later, when Goldschmidt had countered their logical
and rational thrusts, and it never failed to destroy Goldschmidt's
position. In a series of political meetings Goldschmidt tried to
point out the danger of incorporating Schleswig into the Danish
kingdom without a vote by the people of Schleswig, but he

failed. The result of the Danish action was the war with Prussia and Schleswig-Holstein (1848–1851).

In 1848 Goldschmidt's personal life was also deeply troubled. He had finally married Johanne Sonne, and she proved to be a burden. Goldschmidt apparently rarely referred to her in speaking or in writing, but he did support her and the daughter as well as he was able, largely through the good offices of his friend, the publisher A. F. Høst (1811–1897).

Goldschmidt had promised his Norwegian friends Andreas and Charlotte Munch a visit, but the political situation and the outbreak of the war in 1848 prevented the trip that year. In 1849 he decided to go. He had long been attracted to Norway, and his friendship with Charlotte had quickened his interest in making the trip. He had corresponded with the Munchs, and had regularly sent Charlotte copies of his periodical *Nord og Syd*. Norway was still closed to Jews, and Goldschmidt had to obtain the humiliating official letter of authorization in order to enter the country. On 3 July 1849 he landed in Christiania (Oslo), and was met by the Munchs, who were accompanied by Jørgen Moe (1813–1882), who with P. Chr. Asbjørnsen (1812–1885) was to become world famous through their collections of Norwegian folk tales. Goldschmidt was much sought after, and among the friends he made in Christiania were the Norwegian poet Johan Sebastian Welhaven (1803–1873) and the Danish writer Jens Hostrup (1818–1892). With the latter, Goldschmidt attended the theater in Christiania, where they saw two of Hostrup's own plays with the actors Adolph Rosenkilde (1816–1882) and his wife Anna (1825–1885). Goldschmidt later visited the Rosenkildes, and was to become hopelessly infatuated with Anna when they met again in Vienna in 1855.

After a week of social life in Christiania, Goldschmidt went on a tour in the mountains of Telemark. As usual, his first impressions of the new surroundings were negative, but—again as usual—his mood soon changed to one of enthusiasm. No small factor contributing to the enchantment of the Norwegian mountain region was his finding in a farmhouse several numbers of *Corsaren,* with a list of local subscribers from the year 1844.

On his mountain tour, Goldschmidt had to stay overnight in private homes, and at the home of a pastor in the Hitterdal

he was profoundly affected by the beauty of the lady of the
house. Although he left the following day, the erotically shaded
memory of the pastor's wife, fused with a folktale motif from
Asbjørnsen and Moe, resulted in Goldschmidt's own "huldre"
tale (a "huldre" was a sort of wood nymph or fairy of Norwegian
folklore) which he published in *Nord og Syd* in 1849 and reworked in English for *The Victoria Magazine,* where it was
published in 1868.

Following his mountain tour, Goldschmidt returned to Christiania, where he was a frequent guest of Welhaven. Once while
Goldschmidt was visiting Welhaven, King Oscar I came to
call, and Goldschmidt was granted an audience with the king.
Among other leading Norwegians whom Goldschmidt met was
the Landsmaal poet and journalist Aasmund Olafsson Vinje
(1818–1870).

Goldschmidt's first visit to Norway lasted only a month, but
it was of considerable intellectual significance for him. He had
discovered the world of the Norwegian folk tale, and his im-
pressionable fantasy had absorbed firsthand its atmosphere.
Goldschmidt promised his Norwegian friends to return soon
to Norway, but this was a promise he did not keep. Charlotte
Munch, the principal attraction to Norway, died the next year,
and Goldschmidt did not return until 1870. But Norway was
frequently reflected in his writings in *Nord og Syd.* Among the
acquaintances he later made among well-known Norwegians
were the writer Bjørnstjerne Bjørnson (1832–1910) and the violin
virtuoso Ole Bull (1810–1880). He was to become good friends
with both, although his friendship with the difficult Bjørnson
blew hot and cold. Incidentally, the first article Goldschmidt
wrote directly in English, without first composing it in Danish,
was an essay on Bull, published in *The Cornhill Magazine*
in 1862.

VII *Renewed Political Activity*

After the adoption of the new Danish constitution, press
restrictions were eased somewhat, and *Nord og Syd* could appear
as a weekly. Goldschmidt was therefore now able to publish
more current commentaries on political affairs. His political

acuity evidently came to the attention of the Danish government, for in 1850 he was sent on a diplomatic mission to Berlin
to participate in the peace negotiations with Prussia. He helped
to compose an appeal, in the Danish king's name, to the people
of Schleswig-Holstein to give up the war in return for autonomy
within the Danish monarchy. His efforts, however, had little
apparent effect. Goldschmidt then went to Paris, by way of
Leipzig and Frankfurt, commissioned to present the Danish side
of the conflict to the international press. Here, too, he was
unsuccessful, since the foreign press releases were controlled
largely by the Germans.

Frustrated in his official endeavors, Goldschmidt put his time
to good use in Paris by studying French political life, which he
described in *Nord og Syd* the same year. In the National
Assembly he saw Victor Hugo participating in a debate, and
this too found its way into *Nord og Syd*. He also became closely
acquainted with the more notorious side of Parisian life, and
this was also reflected in his later writings.

While in Paris, in July 1850, Goldschmidt found the opportunity to make use of the letter of introduction to Heinrich
Heine which he had received three years earlier from Karl
Varnhagen von Ense in Berlin. Goldschmidt reported his meeting with the already fatally ill Heine in *Nord og Syd* in 1851.
Their common cultural and religious heritage provided an
immediate basis for mutual understanding. Since it turned out
that Heine had heard of Goldschmidt's *A Jew*, their discussion
included a summary of its contents by Goldschmidt.

Back in Copenhagen, Goldschmidt resumed his political
activity, directed primarily against the national liberals. He
had always been too broad in outlook to accept all the tenets
of any one party, and he was too honest to ignore the weak-
nesses in all party lines. In 1848 he had participated in the
recently organized "artisans' educational union" ("Haandvær-
kerdannelsesforening"), and in 1850 he was drawn into a new
political organization of wealthy and aristocratic landowners.
A young aristocrat, Baron C. F. Blixen Finecke (1822–1873),
called on him with the proposal that Goldschmidt lend his
support to the new organization, which was trying to gain
political power. The younger landowners had decided that the

author of the political commentaries in *Nord og Syd* would be the ideal mouthpiece for their association. Goldschmidt, the perpetual outsider, was flattered and charmed by Blixen Finecke's offer, and agreed to work with the new group. It is clear that his highly romanticized image of the young aristocrats as enlightened, generous, and democratic philanthropists gravely misled him. He recommended the organization in his periodical, and helped to compose an address to the king on its behalf. But Goldschmidt's association with his new friends did not last long, and he was made to feel the snobbery of the aristocrats directed against him not only as a paid writer, but also as a Jew. His relationship with the aristocrats was dissolved in 1852, with disappointment and bitterness on both sides. Goldschmidt's political opponents seized on the golden opportunity of branding Goldschmidt as a political opportunist and turncoat, without firm principles.

VIII   *England*

In addition to Goldschmidt's disappointments in politics came another of his ambiguous and complicated infatuations. A young woman named Mathilde Fibiger (1830–1872) had published, under the name "Clara Raphael," a literary effort in epistolary form, dealing with women's rights. Goldschmidt reviewed the work in *Nord og Syd;* he found "Clara Raphael's" views exaggerated, but admitted society's prejudices. In response to the review, Goldschmidt received a letter from another young woman, signed "Sibylla," strongly defending the views expressed by "Clara Raphael," and demanding the emancipation of women. In the next number of his periodical, Goldschmidt asked for permission to publish the letter, and this led to an exchange of letters between Goldschmidt and "Sibylla." Her real name was Lodovica de Bretteville (1827–1859); she was the orphaned daughter of a French immigrant living in Copenhagen. As soon as they met, Goldschmidt was in love. He had just taken his five-year-old son to care for, and felt all the more keenly the desire to establish a real family. She was startled by his ardor, and in a new series of letters, now signed "Romana," she attempted to reestablish her distance. They met again at a masquerade, and she agreed to a rendezvous. At the last minute, however, she had second thoughts, and the affair ended there; she later married someone else.

Goldschmidt again healed his wounds by returning to literature. He now decided to return to the novel, the idea for which stemmed from his stay in Rome. He applied to one of his aristocratic landowner friends for a sizeable sum of money—at this time he was still on friendly terms with the group—and it was readily granted. Goldschmidt determined to suspend publication of *Nord og Syd* for a time and go to London, where he had not been before, but where he had relatives.

Since the events of the Napoleonic era, when the British had made off with the Danish navy, the Danes had generally had no liking for England. English was little taught in Danish schools; German and French were the foreign languages and cultures that were cultivated. Goldschmidt, however, had family connections in London—two cousins, Martin Levin (1818–1875) and Benjamin Rothschild (1810–1884). Rothschild (who was not related to the wealthy dynasty from Frankfurt) had made a considerable fortune in the diamond trade and had married an English woman. The Rothschilds were to play an important role in Goldschmidt's life, and Goldschmidt accepted their hospitality repeatedly on visits to London. Rothschild's wife Hester was to be of great help to him in editing his English writings, and it is fairly clear that she and Goldschmidt eventually became lovers.

When Goldschmidt first visited the Rothschilds' home, he wrote to his mother and sister describing Hester, and added that there was no question of his falling in love with her.[5] In view of his susceptibilities in this area, his protestation may be considered suspect. Twenty years later, when the Danish writer Holger Drachmann (1846–1908) visited Goldschmidt at the Rothschilds' home, he wrote that Goldschmidt and Hester were said to be lovers.[6] Among Goldschmidt's unpublished English notes and draft materials preserved in the Royal Library in Copenhagen there are several fragments of letters to him from Hester which certainly indicate strong feelings on her part. Goldschmidt made a practice of burning her letters when he had read them, and these fragments survived, presumably, because they contained information he had requested from her concerning Jewish culture and traditions. Benjamin Rothschild evidently did not discover the relationship between Hester and Goldschmidt, for he and Goldschmidt remained on close terms, and Benjamin expended large sums of money on Goldschmidt.

Goldschmidt arrived in England in July 1851, and felt at home almost at once. His immediate purpose was to visit the Great Exhibition in Hyde Park, which he described in reports later published in his periodical. He was enraptured by the exposition, as well as by the busy life of the huge city. Besides visiting the exposition, he spent some of his time working on *Homeless* and visiting some of the European political exiles living in England, including Arnold Ruge, his old acquaintance from Leipzig, who was then living in Brighton. Goldschmidt was not so concerned with English political life on this first visit, although he was already fascinated with the figure of the Jewish-born Benjamin Disraeli. In contrast to his later custom, he did not make great efforts to meet leading literary figures. Elias Bredsdorff cites the existence of a draft of a letter of introduction for Goldschmidt from Hans Christian Andersen to Charles Dickens, dated 7 July 1851, but there is no evidence that Goldschmidt made use of such a letter.[7]

After a two-month stay in England, Goldschmidt returned to Copenhagen, where he was to be subjected to continued vicious attacks in the press, primarily because of his political association with the young aristocratic landowners. He discovered that the sum of money he had received from them was considered as payment for services to be rendered, rather than as a loan between gentlemen. This exposed him to the accusation of having been bought by the aristocrats, and although he broke with them, he was branded as their lackey.

In January 1852, Goldschmidt was the victim of a malevolent attack by the literate social reformer Frederik Dreier (1827–1853) in a book entitled *M. A. Goldschmidt, et Litteraturbillede* (*M. A. Goldschmidt, a Literary Picture*). By ingeniously quoting Goldschmidt out of context, Dreier made him seem an unprincipled opportunist devoid of convictions. It was well enough done to provide Goldschmidt's critics with ammunition against him for years.

In the summer of 1852, Goldschmidt made his second visit to England, and again stayed with his cousin Benjamin Rothschild. He visited the Isle of Wight, the scenery of which impressed him, and subsequently observed the political life of London. While in London, he frequently called on Frederica Rowan (1814–1882) and Mrs. Anne Bushby (d. 1875), both translators from the Scandinavian languages. Goldschmidt already entertained the idea of breaking into the English book market. In fact, two English translations of his first novel, *A Jew*, appeared in England by 1852, one by Mrs. Bushby, the other by Mary Howitt (1799–1888). (*The Athenæum* published a review of Mary Howitt's translation in its number for 20 December 1851, although the title page bears the date 1852.) The popularity of the novel is attested by the fact that Howitt's translation was reprinted in 1864, and Mrs. Bushby's was issued in a cheap popular series simultaneously with the more expensive edition.

Always interested in social problems, Goldschmidt visited a number of privately financed schools and charitable institutions for the poor, and was struck by the progressive innovations of the English. The schools, as well as numerous travel impressions, were described in *Nord og Syd*.

Of importance to Goldschmidt was his increasing involvement, through the Rothschilds, in the Jewish circles of London. Though he never became orthodox, he developed an intense interest in Jewish cultural life, and on this and subsequent visits to London, he made every effort to broaden his circle of acquaintances among the city's Jewish leaders. This circle came to include the noted philanthropists Sir Isaac Lyon Goldsmid (1778–1859) and Moses Montefiore (1784–1885), as well as the editor of *The Jewish Chronicle*, Dr. Abraham Benisch (1811–1878). Goldschmidt's unorthodox views earned him the hostility of some members of the Jewish community, however, among them Rabbi Aaron Levy Green (1821–1883); and they probably were the cause of Goldschmidt's expulsion from the Rothschilds' home by Benjamin in 1863.

Meanwhile, Goldschmidt's Danish critics, taking their cue from Dreier, who had branded Goldschmidt a writer whose fine sense of style concealed a paucity of ideas, sharpened their attacks. He was caricatured in his old periodical *Corsaren,* and was ridiculed on the Copenhagen stage in comic reviews.

Goldschmidt's involvement with Lodovica de Bretteville was at this time repeating itself with the original "Clara Raphael." Goldschmidt had reviewed another of her literary efforts, this time more favorably, and in September 1853, "Clara"—Mathilde Fibiger—asked him for his help in writing a novel. Goldschmidt visited her, and he was once again trapped in a relationship that ultimately led nowhere. After more than a year (in December 1854), their relationship, whatever its nature, was terminated.

IX   Homeless

From 1853 to 1857, the pages of *Nord og Syd* were largely taken up by Goldschmidt's second novel, *Homeless,* the massive semi-philosophical result of nearly ten years' work. It incorporated long and detailed—at times almost photographic—descriptions of places, people, and events the author had encountered on his grand tour of 1846–1847, especially during his stay in Rome. It was apparently separately published at the same time, and by 1861 it had appeared in both English and German translations. The novel has generally been underestimated and has not been alloted the position it seems to deserve in Danish and world literature.

To reinforce his impressions of popular Catholicism, which plays an important part in the novel, Goldschmidt visited the Rhine region in the summer of 1853. There he saw the famous Lorelei and romantic castle ruins along the Rhine, which later figured in some of his stories. His itinerary included Cologne and Frankfurt.

In 1854 Goldschmidt made another short trip to London which increased his liking for England and the English. During this stay in London he met several of the leading British literary figures of the period, including Dickens, Bulwer Lytton, and Chauncey Hare Townshend (1798–1868),[8] as well as Disraeli.

In 1855 Goldschmidt traveled to Bohemia and Silesia, where he was to study social problems. He went to Vienna, where he visited the actor Adolph Rosenkilde and his wife Anna, whom he had met in Christiania in 1849. He was with them only a few days, but it was long enough for him to fall in love with Anna. He recognized the hopelessness of the situation, however, and voluntarily broke off the relationship. The romance, like most of Goldschmidt's emotional experiences, was sublimated in literature, and appears in an episode of the novel *Homeless.* In 1856 he was again in London and in Paris, where he saw his old friend P. L. Møller.

In 1858 Goldschmidt fell ill with typhoid fever and had to be hospitalized. After his release from the hospital, he turned the editorship of *Nord og Syd* temporarily over to the literary historian Carl Rosenberg (1829–1885), and went south to recover his health. In late December he arrived in Vienna, where he remained only a short time, then went on to Italy. Among the acquaintances he made along the way were the German Jewish writer Berthold Auerbach (1812–1882) and the director of the *Burgtheater* in Vienna, Heinrich Laube (1806–1884). In Venice he met Richard Wagner, whose music he accepted with reservation. In Vienna and in Milan, his next stop, he saw preparations for war, and these impressions, as usual, were reflected in his writing, this time in his later novel *Arvingen* (*The Heir*). By mid-1859 he was back in Copenhagen.

Later in 1859 Goldschmidt went to London to arrange for an English translation of *Homeless.* Benjamin Rothschild agreed to subsidize the publication, and the English version appeared in 1861 entitled *Homeless, or a Poet's Inner Life.* With the two translations of *A Jew* which had appeared nearly ten years earlier, it would, Goldschmidt hoped, make his name with the English reading public.

The contents of *Nord og Syd* had over the years become more and more literary; in addition to the novel *Homeless*, it was filling up with short stories and literary criticism, at the expense of commentary on social and political questions. Goldschmidt lost subscribers as a result of the serialized novel, and the difficulties of keeping the journal going single-handedly since 1848, despite his illness and his many trips abroad, were telling on him. In May 1860, after concluding the previous year's volume, he decided to cease publication. Twelve years of writing and editing a journal of the level of *Nord og Syd* represents a prodigious achievement. Coupled with Goldschmidt's production of a different nature in *Corsaren,* this secures his name in the history of journalism, just as his novels and short stories ensure him a certain place in the history of world literature.

In 1860 Benjamin Rothschild invited Goldschmidt to accompany him as an interpreter on a business trip to Paris, Geneva, and northern Italy. In Geneva Goldschmidt was recognized and greeted on the street by Hans Christian Andersen, who accompanied him and Rothschild back to their hotel, where Andersen proceeded to bore and irritate Goldschmidt by talking constantly about himself and his own works.

When he returned to Copenhagen, apparently in late 1860, Goldschmidt decided to start a new weekly, *Hjemme og Ude* (*At Home and Abroad*). The new venture was to last only one year, however. Goldschmidt became actively involved, for the last time, in politics. A new political organization, "Dannevirke," had just been established to try to force the Danish government to adopt a more aggressive attitude toward Prussia. Goldschmidt himself felt that if war was inevitable, Denmark should take the initiative, rather than waiting until Prussia was fully prepared for it. Once again, Goldschmidt was probably right, but once again his advice went unheeded. Recognizing that this was his final political defeat, the disillusioned Goldschmidt, who was, moreover, overwhelmed by debts, once more took refuge in London with his cousin Benjamin Rothschild, after having turned *Hjemme og Ude* over to another cousin, Joseph Michaelsen (1826–1908).

Goldschmidt was almost forty-two years old when he went to England in August 1861. He seems to have felt that Denmark had turned its back on him, and he in turn had decided that he was leaving Denmark for good. Since he could not seem to make his name in Danish literature, he had resolved on the daring and risky step of trying to gain fame as an English writer. A brilliant linguist, he had already achieved an excellent command of French, Italian, and German. He had performed efficiently as his cousin's interpreter and translator, and his English was nearing perfection. It remained to be seen, of course, whether his sense of style in the use of Danish would carry over to his written English.

How much of the English version of *Homeless* is in Gold-schmidt's own English is not completely clear. Frederica Maclean Rowan, a well-known translator, apparently began the translation but did not continue it, and Goldschmidt thanked Hester Rothschild for her assistance in a dedication, while Rowan is nowhere mentioned in the English version. Hester evidently knew no Danish, so her aid must have been limited to editorial revision. The English version seems therefore, to a great extent, to have been Goldschmidt's own work. There are substantial differences between the Danish and English versions; the English one is superior in a general tightening of the whole structure, and the changes suggest that Goldschmidt was writing directly in English.

It has generally been the fashion for Danish literary historians to ignore the months Goldschmidt spent in England (August 1861–January 1863) as practically barren in his literary production, and to emphasize that he was under great psychological pressure and suffering constantly from homesickness for Copenhagen. An examination of his letters from England to his family and those he later wrote from Rome to the Rothschilds, as well as of his published English writings and unpublished English notes in the Royal Library, however, demonstrates that he was extremely active literarily, that he was by no means squandering his talents, and that he was enjoying himself hugely as the visiting relative of a millionaire. He met many of the leading English men of letters and publishers, moved in intellectual circles as an accepted and respected member, and especially enjoyed discussing Jewish traditions and culture among the London Jewish community. He published articles and short stories in many of the leading English periodicals of the day, including *Macmillan's Magazine*, *The Cornhill Magazine*, and *Chambers's Journal*, and became acquainted with many of London's publishers, including David Masson (1822–1907), Robert Chambers (1802–1871), and Emily Faithfull (1836–1895).

Goldschmidt had abandoned Danish politics, and his attitude had changed to such an extent that he even began sending articles to his old enemy *Fædrelandet*. Among these articles was a report of a meeting of a delegation of Danish workers which had come to London in 1862 to see the world exposition in the Crystal Palace. The Danish colony had met to honor the delegation, and Goldschmidt was invited to speak under the Danish flag. This scene, which Goldschmidt later described in his autobiography, he poeticized into a crucial point in his life; he later read into it a symbolic reconciliation between himself and Denmark, a sign that he should return home. The description becomes a little absurd and loses a great deal of its subsequently acquired poetic aura when one realizes that another year passed before Goldschmidt did in actual fact return to Denmark, but Goldschmidt's biographers have taken the incident seriously, and date his decision to give up his English writing from it. The fact is that his English writing was just getting into full swing at that time, and his ambition to make his name as a writer in England was unabated.

At this time Goldschmidt's interest in the theater intensified. He was a regular theatergoer in London and was especially impressed by the Shakespeare performances he attended. With support from the "Selskab for de skjønne Videnskaber" (Society for the Arts), he published two dramatic works of his own in Copenhagen—*Rabbi Eliezer* (1861) and *Svedenborgs Ungdom* (*Swedenborg's Youth*) (1863). He also kept abreast of contemporary theater in London, and conceived the idea of translating new English plays and sending them home to Copenhagen to be performed there. The popular comedies and farces of Tom Taylor (1817–1880), Augustus Septimus Mayhew (1826–1875), and Henry Sutherland Edwards (1828–1906) attracted his attention. Taylor had many careers in his lifetime, including that of professor of English literature at London University, art critic for the London *Times*, and editor of *Punch*, but he was best known as a dramatist, and particularly as the author of domestic comedies; he wrote more than seventy plays in thirty-five years, and was one of the most popular playwrights of his time. Goldschmidt translated two of his plays into Danish—*Payable on Demand*, first performed in 1859, and *Up at the Hills*, first performed in 1860. Both of Goldschmidt's translations were accepted and staged by Copenhagen theaters, the latter by the Royal Theater. *Payable on Demand* was based on a legendary version of the rise of the Frankfurt Rothschild dynasty, and this was probably what first attracted Goldschmidt's attention. The motif of the Jew married to a Christian woman (the characters Reuben Goldsched and Lina in the play) may have influenced Goldschmidt's *Rabbi Eliezer,* which was later reworked into the three-act *Rabbi'en og Ridderen* (*The Rabbi and the Knight*). *Payable on Demand* was not an outstanding work, but the brilliant performance of "Frederick Robson" (Thomas Robson Brownhill, ca. 1822–1864), the greatest English comic actor of his day, in the leading role made it one of the five most popular plays of the 1859 season. *Up at the Hills,* however, was not a notable success.

Edwards, too, had a distinguished career. He was a London journalist who had served on the staff of *Punch,* and had been a foreign correspondent for the *Illustrated Times* and the London *Times.* He and Mayhew, who was at one time the editor of *The Comic Almanac,* collaborated on six plays altogether. Goldschmidt translated their one-act farce *The Goose with the Golden Eggs,* which had its first performance in 1859; his translation was accepted and staged by the *Folketeater* in Copenhagen.

Goldschmidt's theatrical concerns, particularly his translations from English into Danish, were of secondary importance to him at this time. He was primarily involved in revising and reworking some of his short stories in English, and in writing articles for English periodicals. In 1862 he published an English version of some of his travel sketches, entitled "On the Danube, and Among the Mountains," in *Chambers's Journal,* as well as his article on Ole Bull, which appeared in *The Cornhill Magazine.* Bull visited Goldschmidt unexpectedly in January 1862 at the Rothschilds' home in London, to the delight of Goldschmidt's hosts and acquaintances.

In October 1862, *Chambers's Journal* printed several of Goldschmidt's "Hebrew Legends," the Danish versions of some of which had appeared in *Nord og Syd.* One of the legends, however—"The Bird that sang to a Bridegroom"—was written originally in English, and Goldschmidt later reworked it in Danish and published it as one of his *Kjærlighedshistorier fra mange Lande* (*Love Stories from many Lands*). This example typifies the complex relationship between Goldschmidt's English and Danish writings. Goldschmidt continued to publish in English, and in January 1863 *Chambers's Journal* printed the English

version of "Aron og Esther," which had appeared in Danish in
1846 in *Stories.* Goldschmidt excitedly wrote to his family that
Robert Chambers, one of the editors of *Chambers's Journal,* had
told him that he had broken a new path in English literature.[9]
In the same letter Goldschmidt mentioned that he had begun a
draft of a "Jewish novel" in English which Chambers would
publish.

Although Goldschmidt's stories continued to appear in English
journals for several years, in January of 1863 he left London
for Rome. It has seemed puzzling that he should suddenly leave
England just at the moment he was making his "breakthrough"
in English letters. His Danish biographers, basing their explana-
tion on Goldschmidt's own highly romanticized account of his
decision, have been content to pass on the following poeticized
story: one foggy winter evening Goldschmidt and Hester Rothschild were sitting by the fireplace, and Hester happened to
mention that some friends were planning to go to Rome. Goldschmidt was at once seized by an uncontrollable yearning to see
Rome again, and left almost immediately, with his travel expenses
being paid by Benjamin Rothschild.

The truth, however, is somewhat different. The details of
Goldschmidt's sudden flight from London are still obscure,
but a close reading of his letters in English to the Rothschilds
from Rome, coupled with an examination of the draft material
for his English novel—which, as usual, is autobiographical—
pieces together the following circumstances surrounding his
abrupt departure: Goldschmidt and Benjamin had indeed talked
earlier of going to Rome together, and Benjamin had left on a
business trip to Paris, with the understanding that Goldschmidt
and he might go to Rome when Benjamin returned. While in
Paris, Benjamin apparently received a letter from certain members of the London Jewish community—probably Rabbi Aaron
Levy Green of the Old Portland Street Synagogue ("Aaron
White" in the unpublished notes for the English novel) and
Barnett Meyers (1814–1889), a wealthy manufacturer of um-
brellas and canes and a donor to the Jews' College (which
Green had had a leading role in founding, and on the board of
directors of which Benjamin Rothschild, also a donor, sat). The
letter demanded that Goldschmidt be expelled from the Roth-

schilds' home. This caused Benjamin in turn to write Goldschmidt a mysterious letter—"letter of exile," as Goldschmidt called it —and Goldschmidt, without waiting for Benjamin's return, hurriedly packed and departed. The fact that Benjamin did pay Goldschmidt's travel expenses and his debts in Denmark would seem to indicate that Goldschmidt's relationship with Hester did not figure in Goldschmidt's expulsion. A more probable reason involves Goldschmidt's liberal and unorthodox views on Judaism, especially his preoccupation with the historical figure of Christ and his admiration for certain other aspects of the Christian philosophy. These views brought him into sharp conflict with various influential and prominent members of the London Jewish community, including, beside Green and Meyers, Abraham Benisch, the influential editor of *The Jewish Chronicle*, a Zionist and rather fanatical anti-Christian, and Jacob Abraham Franklin (1809–1877), a strict orthodox opponent of all reform movements in Judaism, and a contributor to Benisch's newspaper. Both Benisch and Franklin figure by name in the notes for the English novel. Whatever the details of the affair, the incident hurt Goldschmidt deeply, and he was understandably left with a lasting feeling of bitterness toward these men. In a letter to Hester from Rome, dated 7 March 1863, Goldschmidt alluded to the hostile group in London and added, "I further thank God, that there is a novel to describe them in."[10]

In Rome, where Goldschmidt stayed from February till May 1863, there were so many Scandinavians that they formed a small colony and had their own organizations—the official Scandinavian Union ("Den skandinaviske Forening") and the unofficial "Society of Virtue" ("Dydsforening"). Among the notable Scandinavians with whom Goldschmidt became acquainted in Rome were the Norwegians Lorentz Dietrichson (literary and art historian, 1834–1917) and his wife Mathilde (1837–1921), and Ole Henriksen Fladager (sculptor, 1832–1871); the Danes Kristian Arentzen (literary historian, 1823–1899), Carl Frederik Holbech (sculptor, 1811–1880), Vilhelm Bergsøe (writer, 1835–1911), August Saabye (sculptor, 1823–1916), Henrik Olrik (painter, 1830–1890), Valdemar Schmidt (Egyptologist, 1836–1925), and Peter M. Stilling (philosopher, 1812–1869) and his wife Christiane Louise (1832–1903); and the

Swedish painter Mårten Eskil Winge (1825–1896). Goldschmidt
was also acquainted with the English-born writer and linguist
Maria Espérance von Schwartz ("Elpis Melena," 1818–1899),
who became famous through her association with Garibaldi, and
who at that time maintained a kind of literary salon in her home
in Rome, where Goldschmidt has one of his stories ("En Soirée,"
1865) take place. Largely because of the stimulating associations
which Goldschmidt cultivated, the months he spent in Rome
were among the most productive as well as the most enjoyable,
of his life.

Goldschmidt spent much of his time in Rome in the company
of the members of the "Society of Virtue," which, according to
Goldschmidt, took its name from the fact that its members
recognized the virtue of drinking only good wine. They con-
vened in various taverns, and had no fixed meeting place.
Goldschmidt described the "Society" in his "Hvorledes man
lever i Rom" ("How they live in Rome" [1863]). Vilhelm
Bergsøe also described it in his book *Eventyr i Udlandet* (*Adven-
ture Abroad* [1905]). Both Bergsøe and Dietrichson wrote of
Goldschmidt in Rome, the latter in his *Svundne Tider* (*Bygone
Times* [1901]). Both described visits, in Goldschmidt's company,
to the ghetto in Rome, where Goldschmidt's emotional experience of 1847 was repeated, and where he attended a synagogue
service that impressed him deeply.

Almost predictably, Goldschmidt fell in love in Rome. The
object of his feeling this time was Christiane Stilling. Half
Jewish by birth (undoubtedly an added mystical attraction for
Goldschmidt), she had been a much sought-after beauty in
Copenhagen. In fact, Goldschmidt himself had been attracted
to her before her marriage to Stilling, by whom she now had
two children. Stilling was suffering from tuberculosis, and was
frequently unable to escort his wife, so the duty of escort fell
upon Goldschmidt. Both Dietrichson and Bergsøe noted his
affection for her, a feeling which was evidently reciprocated.
There has long been a tradition, although little more than a
romantic fiction, that Mrs. Stilling convinced Goldschmidt that
it was his duty to give up his ambition to become a writer of
English and return to Denmark to devote himself to Danish literature. This pretty little story, started by Goldschmidt him-

self, has been passed on by his biographers, but the truth was that Goldschmidt, discouraged by his slow acceptance in England and embittered by the circumstances surrounding his sudden departure from the Rothschilds' home, had probably already decided that his future lay in Denmark. It seems to be true, however, that, as Goldschmidt claimed, Christiane Stilling did provide the inspiration for much of Goldschmidt's prolific production of the 1860s, although her all-pervasive influence was probably nothing more than a myth, again started by Goldschmidt himself.

Incidentally, Mrs. Stilling had another admirer on the scene in Rome, in the person of the noted German philosopher and professor Kuno Fischer (1824–1907). When Stilling died in 1869, although there were rumors that she and Goldschmidt might marry, Christiane settled the matter by marrying Fischer that same year.

Goldschmidt had taken the notes and drafts for his projected "Jewish novel" in English along with him to Rome, and had been working on it there. As he wrote in a letter to his family, the novel would correct the "error" in *Homeless*, where the hero should have been a Jew.[11] This draft material, preserved in the Royal Library in Copenhagen, indicates that the novel was to be a philosophical work, concerned primarily with the dual problem of the position of the enlightened Jew in an orthodox Jewish milieu, surrounded in turn by a Christian society; and of the artist's pursuit of an unattainable and undefined "ideal." Unfortunately, the novel was abandoned when Goldschmidt decided to return to Denmark. The draft material is of great interest, however, since besides demonstrating Goldschmidt's ability to compose in English, it contains much autobiographical information which casts light on the otherwise rather shadowy period of his stay in England from 1861 to 1863.

X   *Home*

Although Goldschmidt's stay in Rome seems to have meant the abandonment of his hopes and ambitions concerning his becoming an English writer, the inspiration he absorbed there resulted in a series of works during the 1860s which made him the leading Danish writer of the decade. The Danish scholar Knud Wentzel has suggested that Goldschmidt's mastery of style, which reached its peak in the works he produced after his return to Denmark, may have partially resulted from writing in a foreign language and being forced to concentrate heavily on form and style.[12] Goldschmidt's Danish works of this period include *Fortællinger og Skildringer* (*Stories and Descriptions* [1863–1865]), the third volume of which contained the novel *Arvingen* (*The Heir*); *Kjærlighedshistorier fra mange Lande* (*Love Stories from many Lands* [1867]); and *Smaa Fortællinger* (*Little Stories* [1868]), containing the masterpiece "Bjergtagen I" ("Bewitched I").

When Goldschmidt left Rome in May 1863, instead of traveling directly to Copenhagen, he returned briefly to London to see the Rothschilds (his reasons for the detour are not completely clear), and reached Copenhagen in July. In several respects Goldschmidt returned a new man. He no longer had any desire to be a political writer; he was even reconciled with his former political opponents. He was filled with ideas for new works, and his philosophy of Nemesis, his idea of divine justice and order, figured more and more clearly in his works, until he virtually gave up creative writing in the 1880s to devote all his energies to "research" into this religion, as he called it, which had become an obsession. From now on, travel was no longer to be the source of revitalization and inspiration for him; his trips abroad became shorter, and were mainly to England and France, where he often accompanied the Rothschilds, especially Hester, whose health was failing and who frequently visited the resorts of southern France. As Goldschmidt himself aged, his trips were principally to health resorts.

Most of the next two years were spent in Copenhagen, but in the summer of 1865 he "discovered" a part of Denmark previously unknown to him—the northwest coast of Jutland. The fact that Mrs. Stilling had an estate in northern Jutland, and that she had mentioned the area to him while they were together in Rome, may have had something to do with his sudden interest in the region. The excursion, the first of several to the area, resulted in his *Dagbog fra en Reise paa Vestkysten af Vendsyssel og Thy* (*Journal of a Trip on the West Coast of*

Vendsyssel and Thy [areas of northwestern Jutland] [1865]).
In 1866 Goldschmidt repeated his tour of discovery, this time
in central Jutland, the territory of Denmark's foremost provincial writer, Steen Steensen Blicher (1782–1848); the trip was
described in *En Hedereise i Viborg-Egnen* (*A Trip through the
Heath in the Viborg District* [1867]). Another result of the tour
was the psychological novella *Den Vægelsindede paa Graahede*
(*The Fickle Girl on Graahede*) which appeared the same year.

In 1865 Goldschmidt had published an epistolary novella,
Breve fra Choleratiden (*Letters from the Time of Cholera*); the
second edition of 1867 was given the title *En Roman i Breve*
(*A Novel in Letters*). It was built around Goldschmidt's two
favorite themes—the quest for inner harmony (usually associated
with a fantasy of a "perfect" woman), and the purposefulness
of the apparently coincidental. In 1867 Goldschmidt's final novel,
Ravnen (*The Raven*) was printed; it is probably his finest novel
in a structural sense, if not his most interesting. As usual, there
are autobiographical threads running through the story—the
central idea of embezzlement reappears, based on the ruinous
experience of Goldschmidt's father in the loss of his ship. *The
Raven* is important among Goldschmidt's works since it contains
one of the most memorable figures Goldschmidt ever created—
the little Jewish commercial agent Simon Levi. He appealed
to readers—and to Goldschmidt—so much that he appeared in
two further stories.

The same year that *The Raven* appeared (1867), Goldschmidt
was struck by an article on the Talmud in the English *Quarterly
Review,* written by the noted Talmudic scholar and librarian
of the British Museum, Immanuel Deutsch (1819–1873).[13] He
translated and published it anonymously in 1868, and sent a
copy to his friend, the well-known Danish critic Clemens Petersen (1834–1918). Accompanying the translation was a long
letter explaining the significance which the Talmud, and
Jewish culture in general, had had for his own development.
The letter constitutes an important document in the study of
both the life and the works of Goldschmidt.[14] Jewish themes
had always been prominent in Goldschmidt's writings, but
during his final creative period his Jewish stories form a separate
little group, which includes some of his finest creations—"Maser"

(1868), "I en Postvogn" ("In a Stagecoach" [1868]), *Avrohmche Nattergal* (1871), "Levi og Ibald" ("Levi and Ibald" [1883]), and "Mendel Hertz" (1883).

During the 1860s Goldschmidt tried his hand at a new genre—drama. Even during the *Corsaren* period he had written critical articles on the theater—articles which reveal sound principles of dramatic judgment—and he continued his theater criticism in *Nord og Syd*. Goldschmidt's experimentation in the new genre had begun in the 1850s; C. N. Rosenkilde (1786–1861), a noted actor in the Royal Theater, once suggested that Goldschmidt should write for the stage, since the dialogue in his stories demonstrated dramatic talent. In late 1857 Goldschmidt had dashed off a play and sent it to J. L. Heiberg (1791–1860), at that time the "censor" (the official charged with examining each new play submitted, and passing judgment on its acceptability) for the Royal Theater. The play, entitled "Vagabonden" ("The Vagabond"), was rejected, but in 1863 Goldschmidt resubmitted it in a reworked form to Carsten Hauch (1790–1872), who now occupied the post of "censor." Again the play was rejected. During his long stay in England, Goldschmidt had completed another dramatic work, *Rabbi Eliezer* (published in 1861). Apparently Goldschmidt intended to publish an English version, for a translation of a scene from it, written in Goldschmidt's hand, is among his English notes in the Royal Library. *Rabbi Eliezer* was followed, in 1863, by *Svedenborgs Ungdom* (*Swedenborg's Youth*). Neither attracted a great deal of attention.

In the burst of creative activity following his visit to Rome in 1863, Goldschmidt reworked "Vagabonden" and gave it the new title *En Skavank* (*A Flaw*, published in 1867). In 1864, when the Norwegian writer Bjørnstjerne Bjørnson visited him, Goldschmidt showed the play to him. Bjørnson liked it and showed it to Clemens Petersen, who also thought it was good, and on their advice Goldschmidt submitted the play for the third time to the Royal Theater. This time it was accepted, but for some reason it was shelved and not staged, a not uncommon practice at the time on the part of the theater's administration. Goldschmidt protested and finally lodged an official complaint with the ministry, which upheld him and in 1867 ordered that the play be presented. Goldschmidt's official complaint to the ministry was not the result of mere querulousness and egotism. As the theater historian Edgar Collin explained in his continuation of Thomas Overskou's *Den danske Skueplads* (*The Danish Theater*), Goldschmidt's action resulted in the abolition of the longstanding and unauthorized abuse of authors' rights by the administration of the Royal Theater.[15]

In 1869 Goldschmidt had a second play on the stage of the Royal Theater, the two-act comedy *I den anden Verden* (*In the Other World*). It was not a particular success, though it did have seven performances. That same year, however, Goldschmidt's last theatrical work was staged, and this time he had produced a drama deserving of a better fate than it received. This was the three-act *Rabbi'en og Ridderen* (*The Rabbi and the Knight*), a reworking of *Rabbi Eliezer*. The play ran for eight performances, and was well received by the public and by all the critics, with one exception—the young Georg Brandes, later to become Denmark's greatest and most famous critic. Although Brandes also was Jewish by birth, he and Goldschmidt never understood each other, and their relationship was for the most part a rather embittered one. Brandes' review of *The Rabbi and the Knight* included a parodying of the play, a rather cheap but usually effective weapon of critics. The play brought Goldschmidt another unpleasant experience, which ended in the courts. The publisher of the original *Rabbi Eliezer* had lost money on that work, and wanted to publish *The Rabbi and the Knight* and by paying Goldschmidt a low royalty, to recoup his losses. Believing that he had so thoroughly reworked the play that it was now a different work, Goldschmidt sold the work to another publisher. The original publisher sued Goldschmidt, and the court decided in the publisher's favor. Goldschmidt was fined and had to pay court costs.

The early 1870s brought Goldschmidt several saddening blows. In 1870 his mother—an unfailing source of support, of advice, and, at times, of strained patience and irritation—died. It was her wish that Goldschmidt move in with his unmarried sister Ragnhild; Goldschmidt complied, and was for the rest of his life cared for by the devoted Ragnhild. Another shock concerned the death of Carsten Hauch, whom Goldschmidt had visited when Hauch was on his deathbed in Rome in 1872. Taking his leave of the dying man, Goldschmidt had said, "Farvel saalænge" ("Goodbye for now"), possibly implying that they could meet in the hereafter. Goldschmidt published a letter describing the meeting in a Copenhagen newspaper, and included a mention of the emotional leave-taking. To his surprise, this caused a stir in the good Christian society of Copenhagen—the effrontery of a Jew, assuming that he would share eternity with Christians! Someone actually wrote to Hauch's family, asking if they shared this feeling. Although the family denied having any part in this anti-Jewish sentiment, Goldschmidt was understandably disgusted over the petty affair.

Goldschmidt was to be reminded yet again of the anti-Semitism still prevalent in certain circles of Danish society, although it was unquestionably dying out generally. Always on the lookout for the "ideal" this and that, Goldschmidt thought he had found the "ideal" secret society in Freemasonry. In the 1860s he had been accepted in a lodge in France, and when he returned to Denmark, he expected to continue participating in the lodge in Copenhagen. Here, however, he discovered that no Jews were allowed to be regular members. He was finally told that he would be allowed to attend not more than three meetings per year, and then only under the condition that all members present pretended to be ignorant of the fact that he was a Jew. One of the members stated flatly that as long as he lived, no Jew would be a Freemason in Denmark. When Goldschmidt tried to protest to the "brothers," he was threatened with the "secret power" of the fraternity. So much for the high-mindedness of the "ideal" secret society. Since Goldschmidt's time, Denmark has become one of the least anti-Semitic societies in the world, and assimilation has caused the so-called Jewish question to lose its meaning there, particularly in literature. Hans Kyrre fittingly summed up Goldschmidt's relationship to Danish anti-Semitism in his *M. Goldschmidt*: "Goldschmidt is the last Jew in Danish literature, but he also continued to bear the stamp of this his entire life."[16]

During the 1870s and 1880s Goldschmidt devoted his time increasingly to "researches" on his philosophical fixation, "Nemesis." This idea became more and more important in his imaginative writing, and in *The Raven,* for example, it is the core around which the entire work is constructed. This concept meant more to Goldschmidt than the personification of punishment for a transgression; to him it was the spirit of moral order in the universe, the checks and balances which kept both the collective and the individual world on a spiritually even keel. It was the mission of every individual to discover the universal moral order and then to bring himself into harmony with it. No one, apparently, has succeeded in fully understanding the details of Goldschmidt's "religion," and few took him seriously as he spent much of the last fifteen years of his life "researching" in the libraries of Europe, particularly the British Museum. The object of these expended energies was to trace the idea of Nemesis back through the religions of history, to try to discover its origin as some sort of proto-religion. Goldschmidt went as far back as ancient Egypt. Most of the historians, theologians, and Egyptologists whom he consulted treated him as the eccentric dilettante he was.

In 1877 Goldschmidt published his autobiography in two volumes, the second of which is devoted entirely to Nemesis. In fact, the first volume, which took his life story generally only up to about 1847, was written only to illustrate the workings of Nemesis in his own life. For this reason, although, like all his works, it is well written, it must be used by a biographer with a very great deal of caution, since Goldschmidt, possibly unconsciously, remolded the events of his life to conform with his "law" of one cause and one effect. Practically every act in his youth was interpreted as symbolic, a mystical presaging of something to come.

During the 1870s Goldschmidt was a frequent visitor to the British Museum, and one of the librarians he met there was the young Edmund Gosse (1849–1928), who later became a noted writer, translator, and authority on Scandinavian literature. As mentioned earlier, Gosse wrote Goldschmidt's obituary in *The Athenæum,* and there he quoted from a letter Goldschmidt had written to him, in which Goldschmidt explained his work on Nemesis.[17] Goldschmidt, "in his own singularly correct English," as Gosse described it, wrote:

... the aim [of the work on Nemesis] is to prove, through history
and science of language, that all our ideas, the religious ones especially, have grown up like a plant from the simplest roots, and that
the power of life, that has made and makes them grow, is the breath
of God (the Egyptian Num).—The divine breath, that pervades the
Universe and rules all things, was the Egyptian Nemt, the Greek
Nemesis. ... In fact, my life is written solely to show the power of
Nemesis or that living quality of Existence, that developed me to
see and to feel Nemesis, the divine breath.

This was evidently the sum of Goldschmidt's intensive work
during his last years.

Goldschmidt's imaginative writing during the last decade of
his life particularly was much limited by his "researches." In
1877 he published *Fortællinger og Virkelighedsbilleder, ældre
og nye* (*Stories and Pictures of Reality, older and new*); in 1883
Fortællinger og Virkelighedsbilleder, Ny Samling (*Stories and
Pictures of Reality, New Collection*) appeared. Goldschmidt had
prepared a collection *Smaa Skildringer fra Fantasi og fra Virkelighed* (*Small Pictures from Fantasy and from Reality*) to
mark the fiftieth anniversary of his debut as a writer and editor
of the *Nestved Ugeblad*, which had printed its first number in
October 1837. But Goldschmidt died suddenly on 15 August
1887, and the collection was published later that year by his
son.

In spite of Goldschmidt's repeated rejections by various seg-
ments of Danish society because he was a Jew, and in spite of
the difficult and oversensitive personality which he developed in
his later years, his achievements in Danish literature were given
recognition in his lifetime. During the 1860s he was recognized
as Denmark's greatest living prose writer. Although in the 1870s
the "Breakthrough"—the realistic movement led by Georg Brandes—was beginning to depose him, he was still the grand old man
of Danish letters. Among many proofs of recognition was his
being awarded the title of professor by the king in 1875.

Every critic who has written on Goldschmidt has applied the
term "stylist" to the writer. Frederik Dreier and others of Goldschmidt's opponents in the 1850s accused Goldschmidt of using
his mastery of style to mask a lack of ideas. Georg Brandes,
while giving Goldschmidt credit as a stylist in a positive sense,

also once accused him of lacking a philosophy. In an obituary article[18] Brandes called Goldschmidt a master of the language, and added that Goldschmidt was "the first shaper [*Udformer*] of a modern Danish literary prose," and that "his language is the best heritage he leaves to us." Edmund Gosse, who was a friend of Goldschmidt, wrote in his obituary article that "the elegance of his style was so great that critics of authority, and these not prejudiced by any personal liking for the man, have been found to say that no Danish prose is so graceful as that of Goldschmidt."

While there has been universal agreement that Goldschmidt was a master stylist, it has proved difficult to define and analyze this "style." In an 1869 article on Goldschmidt,[19] Brandes defined a prose writer's style as "nothing other than the tone in which he usually speaks . . . the order in which he presents events or thoughts . . . and the tempo in which his prose demands to be read. . . . Good style is nothing other than the art of being read and understood." In a recent Danish literary history, Peter P. Rohde wrote that Goldschmidt was the one "who in his own generation spoke and wrote the Danish language with greatest perfection and insight."[20] He continued, "Goldschmidt is as a stylist simple, clear, sincere, and adept at expressing nuances of emotion. He is always sober, moderate, well-balanced, and has in this respect absorbed decisive impulses from Icelandic saga literature. . . . He abhors the pursuit of effects and the affected image. His stylistic art is the art of naturalness." P. M. Mitchell analyzed Goldschmidt's style in more concrete terms: "He is always lucid and careful in his diction. He excels in exposition and description and avoids the fanciful or the fantastic. His sentences are precise, with many modifying clauses and limiting phrases. He makes no effort to portray spectacular outward events. His characters are affected by particular situations and occurrences, the significance of which is revealed only through the intuition of the author."[21] Others have written on Goldschmidt's style—Mogens Brøndsted has devoted a book to an analysis of Goldschmidt's art[22]—and while there may be a variety of subjective adjectives used to attempt to pinpoint the unique quality of Goldschmidt's talent, there is basic agreement that Goldschmidt was indeed the first real master of modern Danish prose writing. His artistry in handling the Danish language permanently influenced Danish literature, and similarities in style have been found in several of Denmark's greatest writers of more recent times; among them Karen Blixen ("Isak Dinesen," 1885–1962) is generally pointed out as Goldschmidt's greatest heritor.

CHAPTER 2

The Novels

GOLDSCHMIDT'S novels have enjoyed a constant reading public in Denmark, and have a continuing appeal for the modern reader, as is attested by the fact that three of his four novels have been reprinted since 1960. The only novel not to be reprinted recently, *Homeless*, is Goldschmidt's longest and possibly most important for what it has to say about Goldschmidt's views on life (before his Nemesis idea became so dominant) and on the political events of contemporary Europe. The four novels differ radically from each other. The first, *A Jew*, enabled Goldschmidt to rid himself, for a time, of the accumulated bitterness over his treatment by Christian society; *Homeless* was an outlet for the mass of experiences and impressions which had filled him on his travels in 1846–1847; *The Heir* typified his idea of the individual's search for his life's mission; *The Raven* embodied his conviction of the inescapability of Nemesis; but they all depicted attempts—successful or unsuccessful—of the individual to bring himself into harmony with himself and with society.

I A Jew

The genesis of Goldschmidt's first novel, *A Jew*, published in 1845 (the second edition, slightly revised, appeared in 1852), has been discussed (see p. 26 above). The novel stemmed from pent-up bitterness over Goldschmidt's personal experiences with what the Danes call the "little anti-Semitism." It is the story of the withering of a potentially great personality because of the accumulation of countless petty manifestations of anti-Semitism in nineteenth-century Danish society.

As an introductory motto for the novel, Goldschmidt used

61

Genesis 3.15: "And I will put enmity between thee and the woman, and between thy seed and her seed; it shall bruise thy head, and thou shalt bruise his heel." This is the gist of the entire work—the love of the Jewish hero for a Christian girl, their incapability of realizing their love because of the enmity existing between their two worlds, and the resultant destruction of both of them. Goldschmidt rendered the motto visually more effective by giving it in Hebrew, followed by the Danish (the Danish biblical translation is more incisive than that of the King James Version; where the English repeats "bruise" the Danish has "crush" ["knuse"] and "wound" ["saare"]).

A *Jew* is constructed symmetrically. As Mogens Brøndsted, Denmark's leading authority on Goldschmidt, has pointed out,[1] each of the novel's three parts represents a segment of the hero's life; each begins with uncertainty and suspense and ends in a break and a leave-taking. As the introductory motto epitomizes the complete novel, the concluding line (separated from the body of the text in print) distills the personal tragedy of the gradual erosion of the hero's idealism in the spoken epitaph, uttered over his grave by his best friend: "He once believed in eternal poetry and eternal life!"

In order to show the destructive effects of the nineteenth-century Christian environment on an idealistic Jewish personality, Goldschmidt depicted the life of his hero from birth to death. Brøndsted has mentioned that *A Jew* is one of the earliest significant Danish novels which demonstrates the inevitable effects of childhood experiences on the entire future development of an individual.[2] The novel's immediate success is to be ascribed to its portrayal of Jewish society in Denmark—this was the first time Jewish life had been pictured realistically in Danish literature. Prior to the appearance of *A Jew*, Jewish characters in Danish literature had been either ridiculed or idealized; Goldschmidt was the first writer to describe, from the inside, Jewish culture with its ceremonies and with its own particular language (Goldschmidt found it necessary to provide footnotes translating the Yiddish and Hebrew expressions and explaining the rites and ceremonies described in the text). The novel was popular principally among the Christians, however; the Jews themselves had learned from generations of bitter experience that they were

most secure when they attracted as little attention from the
Christians as possible. Goldschmidt's exposé of their private life
and customs understandably made many apprehensive and re-
sentful. Even during Goldschmidt's time, assimilation and acceptance of the Jews in Denmark were proceeding rapidly, and
there was soon to be no "Jewish problem" in Denmark (witness
the Danes' organized rescue of almost the entire Jewish population from the Nazis during the occupation). This does not cancel
out the importance of Goldschmidt's description of the Danish
Jewish society; on the contrary, its historical importance was
heightened, since it preserved a picture of a culture which was
even then disappearing. Anja Nathan has demonstrated that
Goldschmidt's descriptions of Jewish life and culture in Denmark
at the time were generally correct and accurate, although he
might occasionally emphasize one aspect at the expense of
another in order to make his point.[3]

The novel's central character, Jacob Bendixen, is born in a
provincial town (as was Goldschmidt himself), in 1808, at the
time the Spanish troops sent to Denmark by Napoleon were
deserting to the British, and Jews were being jeered at for not
bearing arms (though their admission to military ranks was
severely restricted). At an early age Jacob is exposed to the
taunts and persecutions of the Christian children with whom he
wants to play (unlike Goldschmidt as a child). There are too
few Jews in the provincial town to form an organized community
(as was the case in Vordingborg, where Goldschmidt was born),
and there are no other Jewish children close by. Jacob therefore
spends his childhood alone, especially after he almost kills a
Christian boy who has been persecuting him, and his father
is ordered to build a board fence around the garden where
Jacob plays. From then on, Jacob plays alone, compelled to be
a remote spectator to the games of the Christian children. This
increases his sense of permanent physical and psychological
isolation from the Christian world, which haunts him throughout
his life and crystallizes his love-hate relationship with Christian
society.

It is, of course, dangerous to seek too many exact parallels
between Jacob Bendixen and Meïr Goldschmidt, but the novel is
in fact psychologically autobiographical, if not completely so in

reality. Further, as has been indicated, Goldschmidt also was frequently more truthfully autobiographic in his fiction than in his memoirs. Many of the characters in A Jew were based on Goldschmidt's relatives and acquaintances, and many incidents in Jacob's life also occurred in Goldschmidt's. Jacob's uncle, Isak Bamberger, is an artistic portrait of Goldschmidt's own uncle (Isac Meyer, 1772–1860), and Isak's characterization as a powerfully built, belligerent, and physically courageous man—all extremely unusual characteristics for a Danish Jew of the time—mirrors the personality of Goldschmidt's uncle. Jacob's mother, too, resembles Goldschmidt's mother. According to the writer, his own mother sang Danish—not Yiddish—songs to him, just as Jacob's mother does. In each case, this somehow awakened in the boy a vague yearning toward a blond, blue-eyed world.

The anti-Jewish riots which spread into Denmark from Germany in 1819 (shortly before Goldschmidt was born) leave a permanent scar on Jacob. Although the town police official disperses the mob before the Christians can attack Jacob's family and complete the looting of the family businesses (again reflecting an actual occurrence), young Jacob stabs a leader of the mob, but since the latter thinks he has been wounded by the Jewish god, only the family knows of Jacob's act. As the uncle says, "There is now blood between him and the Christians;" this portends the barriers that will separate Jacob from the Christians. At Jacob's bar mitzvah, the passage of the Torah which chance has determined he should read contains the same passage Goldschmidt used as the motto to introduce the novel. This is an author's device, to be interpreted by the reader as a prophetic symbol, but it also reflects a cultural tradition among Jews so to interpret the passage read by a boy at his bar mitzvah. Goldschmidt adds another bad omen—when Jacob is to return to his seat, he starts to leave the platform the wrong way, and must be led in the prescribed direction. In this, too, Goldschmidt was following the characteristic Jewish cultural trait of seeing omens in chance occurrences in rituals. Incidentally, Jacob's mistake in leaving the platform repeated Goldschmidt's own error during his bar mitzvah.

Jacob's father decides to send him to Copenhagen to a school preparing boys for the university. Earlier, Jacob had played war games with a cat—he had no other playmates—and he had ended by killing the cat with a knife. When his father found him, he explained his killing the animal by saying he wanted to see what was inside it. His father interpreted this as a sign that Jacob should study medicine and surgery, and therefore must go to Copenhagen to prepare himself for the university. Jacob's experiences at the school in Copenhagen parallel Goldschmidt's own. The persecutions by the other boys, the humane and just director, and Jacob's superior performance as a pupil are all taken from Goldschmidt's own life. The enlightened director indirectly influences Jacob to begin abandoning the multitude of daily rituals which pervaded the life of the orthodox Jew; this is the beginning of Jacob's "fall." Like Goldschmidt, Jacob is drawn toward the tenets of Christianity, but again like Goldschmidt, he is always to stop short of conversion. When Jacob returns home after finishing school, his father finds out that Jacob has abandoned some of the most hallowed daily rituals, no longer wears the obligatory sacred undergarment, and has even eaten food that was not kosher. His father pronounces a dreaded ritualistic curse over Jacob, and his uncle Isak strikes him. The bonds with his family completely severed, Jacob returns to Copenhagen to enter the university.

The second part of the novel begins with Jacob's having passed his university entry examination with honors. He meets and makes friends with Martin Levy, an advanced medical student, like Jacob an enlightened Jew, but unlike Jacob possessing realistic, almost cynical views on the relationships between Jew and Christian. Levy's character counterbalances Jacob's—Levy has met Christian society and has compromised with it. As he points out to Jacob, he has no independent means, and therefore he must depend largely on Christians for a successful career. He is an "amphibian," as he puts it; he moves easily in both Jewish and Christian circles, though he prefers to avoid any gathering containing members of both societies, and he declares that he would never marry a gentile.

Jacob meets Thora Fangel, the sister of a student friend, and falls in love with her. (The name "Thora" combines the two sides of Jacob's character which are pulling him in opposite directions—the Torah or Pentateuch and the whole of Jewish

law on the one hand, and the Scandinavian heroic mythological
background on the other.) Thora and Jacob become engaged,
and Goldschmidt takes pains to show that the difficulties that
inevitably arise between Jacob and the Fangels' Christian friends
and relatives are partly to be blamed on Jacob himself—he is
morbidly oversensitive and constantly sees insults where none are
intended. Thora's father has nothing against the engagement at
first, but Jacob's erratic behavior in society causes anger and
hurt feelings in the whole family. The family, and eventually
Thora herself, are thus prepared for the insidious influence of
a sanctimonious aunt, the wife of a Lutheran clergyman, who
takes it upon herself to convince the Fangel family that Jacob
must be persuaded to convert to Christianity, which will make
him quite acceptable to Aunt Mathilde and consequently to all
good Christians. Eventually Thora does suggest to Jacob that
he allow himself to be baptized, with disastrous results for
their relationship. Levy also cold-bloodedly suggests the same
course as a prerequisite for a successful marriage to a gentile,
but Jacob always violently rejects the proposal; Jewish culture
and tradition have too strong a hold on him to permit the re-
nunciation of his ancestry and his entire background. The
situation is made worse by the presence of a Lieutenant Engberg,
a would-be suitor of Thora's. When Jacob surprises Thora and
Engberg together, he challenges Engberg to a duel, but Engberg
refuses on the grounds that a gentleman cannot fight a duel
with a Jew. Jacob almost literally throws him out the door,
then leaves the house himself. From other students he learns
of the outbreak of a revolution in France, and decides impulsively to go to Paris to take part in the fighting. He writes
to Thora, expecting her to wait for him after all, and concludes
his letter by passing on to her a blessing he had once received
from his father, before his break with his family. Since Christian
tradition does not attach the importance to a blessing or curse,
nor to the power of the word in general, that Jewish culture
does, the Fangel family simply does not grasp the depth of
meaning which this blessing has for Jacob.

The novel's third part begins with Jacob's arrival in Paris.
He has arrived too late, however, to participate in the revolution,
and wanders aimlessly, vainly expecting a letter of apology and

understanding from Thora. He has a meaningless affair with a French actress (modeled on a similar affair which Goldschmidt had had in Paris), and decides to enlist in the French army in Algeria, to attain the officer's rank denied to Jews in Denmark.

In his garrison in Algeria, Jacob's closest friend is the Polish expatriate Josinski, whose one dream is to fight for Poland's liberation from Russia. On the eve of his first battle with the Bedouins, Jacob receives a letter from Denmark notifying him of his father's death. Remembering his father's (and every orthodox Jew's) dread of dying without having a son to say *Kaddish* for him, since he had repudiated Jacob with his curse, Jacob recites it aloud in his tent. The following day Jacob goes into battle, but when he suddenly sees a line of dark, bearded Bedouins dressed in white burnooses rise from a ditch to face the French soldiers, he is reminded of Jews in a synagogue on Yom Kippur, each in his long white *kittel*, a garment in which the orthodox Jew was also buried, and he is unable to bring himself to fire on them. This picture has been unjustly derided by some critics; in actual fact it is not implausible, but has a certain power, especially as it is rendered simply and in a few words.

As a result of his apparent cowardice, Jacob is involved in a duel with another officer, whom he kills. He thereby regains the respect of Josinski, and their close friendship continues. Jacob discovers some Danish translations of Icelandic sagas in his luggage, and tells Josinski of the Old Norse heroes. (Goldschmidt himself was fascinated by the sagas, and his narrative style may have been influenced by the clear, matter-of-fact style of the saga writers.)

News of the Polish uprising against Russia arrives, and Josinski decides to leave Algeria to return to Poland to fight; on the spur of the moment Jacob determines to accompany him. In Poland Jacob participates in several battles, acquits himself honorably, and is promoted. During the campaign he encounters the sinister figure of a forcibly baptized Jew who has been given the Christian name of Michael Wucziewicz, and saves him from being hanged as a spy. The strange, terrible story of the Jew who has been baptized against his will so that a local Polish official can then take his wife (a baptized Christian could not be married to a Jewish woman) is gradually revealed. The man's children are killed by Russians and he takes his revenge on both sides by spying for each. When Jacob and Josinski are cut off by the Russian forces, Wucziewicz leads them, disguised in the uniforms of two Russians he has killed, through the lines to Warsaw.

In Warsaw Jacob learns that Benjamin, his father's clerk, has come to Poland looking for him. Benjamin is dying of cholera, but before he dies he gives Jacob a letter from Levy announcing Thora's marriage to Jacob's old enemy, Lieutenant Engberg. Immediately thereafter, in a battle resulting in the defeat of the Poles, Jacob is seriously wounded. Josinski rescues him and they eventually reach the border, where they separate.

Back in Copenhagen, Jacob is warmly greeted by his student friends and by Levy, but the latter is on the point of leaving on a study trip to Sweden. When Jacob goes toward Thora's and Engberg's house one evening, he witnesses a rendezvous between Thora and another lieutenant, Grabow. Shattered, Jacob returns home unrecognized. Later, Jacob meets this same Grabow, who asks him for a loan to pay for his portrait, intended as a gift for his mistress, obviously Thora. Jacob agrees to lend him the money on the condition that he can include a note with the portrait. He writes that he had witnessed her tryst with Grabow. Jacob later learns that the shock of learning that he had returned and witnessed her love-making with Grabow, has brought on a collapse and that she has died in a delirium.

In the meantime, Jacob's university friends have learned of his lending money to the young officer and to one of the latter's friends, and misunderstanding Jacob's motives, insult him and expel him from their group, on the assumption that Jacob has become the stereotyped Jewish usurer. Thus his last bonds with the Christian world are violently broken, and he ends by becoming what they thought he was—a ruthless moneylender.

The final chapter, which Goldschmidt said was written first, is Goldschmidt at his narrative best. Without a transition from the preceding chapter, it begins with a description of a Jewish funeral typical of the mid-nineteenth century in Denmark, before the reform movement introduced strict, dignified regulations into the funeral ceremonies. Poor Jews, most of them unacquainted with the deceased, would push their way into the overcrowded carriages making up the funeral procession, in the hope of getting the alms handed out at the cemetery. The whole process was shamefully noisy and totally lacking in dignity and respect. Furthermore, it always attracted the attention of anti-Semitic Christians, who would assemble to shout insults and throw stones at the Jews.

The conversation of a typical carriageful of such Jews on the way to the cemetery is depicted. One of them was acquainted with the deceased, who turns out to be Jacob Bendixen, and Jacob's last days are described. He had turned into a fanatically anti-Christian usurer, who went to great lengths to prevent Jewish boys from studying in Christian schools and from fraternizing with Christians in any way. As a result of the cruel rejection of all his attempts to be accepted into Christian society, he had become a member of the profession which the Christians hated most, and which they considered typical of Jews. He, who had been cursed by his own father for abandoning the trappings of the Jewish faith in his attempt to compromise with Christianity, had become the epitome of what had been to him the most repugnant feature of Jewish society. When Martin Levy had returned home from Sweden, he had met Jacob in the synagogue on Yom Kippur, where they had exchanged a few words of two-edged meaning, quoted but not understood by one of the Jews in the carriage. Jacob collapsed and had to be carried home, where he soon died—of an old war wound, according to the Jew in the carriage. He had died uttering Thora's name, and this was naturally understood by the Jews to mean the holy law, the Pentateuch—Goldschmidt's final touch underlining the duality of Jacob's nature, even at the moment of his death.

After the burial ceremony, which is accompanied by the howls of the Christian mob outside the cemetery (a stone lands on the coffin—the last insult to Jacob from the Christian world), Levy is left alone at the grave, where he pronounces Jacob's epitaph, citing Jacob's own words, uttered years before when Jacob had hopes of breaking down the barriers between Judaism and Christianity: "He once believed in eternal poetry and eternal life!"

A Jew soon acquired for Goldschmidt a fame far different from the kind he had earlier achieved through his writing and editing the satiric journal *Corsaren*. He had proved that he was a serious writer, and could sustain his talent through a full-length novel. *A Jew* has been translated into English (two different translations, 1852), German (1856), Yiddish (1919), and Russian (1919). The English translations have a history of their own. Both were made by women who had translated Hans Christian Andersen—Mrs. Mary Howitt and Mrs. Anne S. Bushby. Mary Howitt had been the first to translate Andersen into English. Although both her translation of *A Jew* and Mrs. Bushby's are dated 1852, Mrs. Howitt's was apparently actually published the year before (see p. 41 above). Mrs. Bushby claims, in her preface, that her translation, entitled *The Jew of Denmark,* had been made "from the original Danish" much earlier, but that its publication had been delayed. She adds that it had Goldschmidt's approval. Mrs. Howitt admits on her title page (her translation was entitled *Jacob Bendixen, the Jew*) that her translation is "adapted from the Danish of Goldschmidt" (curiously, the 1864 reprint of Mrs. Howitt's translation omits the word "adapted" from the title page). The fact that Mrs. Howitt's translation was reprinted and that Mrs. Bushby's translation was issued in both a relatively expensive edition and a cheap popular series attests the novel's popularity in England. Hans Christian Andersen, in a letter written in September 1852 from Copenhagen to Richard Bentley (1794–1871), the publisher of Howitt's translation, mentioned a Danish review of Mrs. Howitt's translation in which it was stated that twenty thousand copies had been sold. Bentley replied, however, in a letter dated 4 October 1852, that there had been no such large sale.[4] The popularity of the English versions was achieved in spite of the fact that neither Mrs. Howitt nor Mrs. Bushby was very competent in Danish, however, and both translations are extremely poor. Andersen, incidentally, was advised by his friend the banker Joseph Hambro (1780–1848) not to authorize Mrs. Howitt as his translator; Hambro called Mr. and Mrs. Howitt a "translation factory."[5] Mrs. Howitt broke off relations with Andersen, and got her revenge later by spreading the rumor that Andersen did not even know Danish well![6]

A curious footnote to Goldschmidt's reaction to the English translations of *A Jew* is his statement in his autobiography that Mrs. Howitt, a Quaker, had indeed "adapted" the novel and had gone so far as to alter it after her own taste to the extent that she had baptized Jacob in the last chapter. Goldschmidt added that this had given him the reputation among English Jews of being a renegade and advocating the baptism of Jews. He went on to say that Mrs. Bushby's more honest translation was more popular and was sold as "railway literature" in both England and America.[7] While Mrs. Howitt was probably entirely capable of taking it upon herself to "improve" a work in this manner, the examples of both editions of her translation which have been accessible for examination reveal no baptism of the hero in the last chapter. By the 1860s Goldschmidt possessed a mastery of English, and he had enough natural vanity to have had the desire to examine the translations firsthand. His many stays in England would have given him the opportunity to do this, so his flat statement gives rise to a little mystery. Richard Bentley, in his letter to Hans Christian Andersen mentioned above, wrote that Howitt's translation had been reprinted during the year of its first appearance, so it is possible that the first printing of that year contained the baptism, and that this addition was later dropped, but evidence to this effect is lacking.

Notwithstanding the success of Goldschmidt's first novel and the lasting interest it possesses, there has been considerable negative criticism directed at it. The lack of depth in development of several of the characters, deficient psychological motivation, loose composition, and superfluous battle scenes have all been deplored. Some of these criticisms are valid; this is not surprising since *A Jew* was a first novel by a writer who had previously been known only as a journalist and satirist. Lack of depth in development and insufficient motivation are valid criticisms, but as Mogens Brøndsted has indicated, the structure of the novel does possess symmetry; and the story does have a certain inevitability. Goldschmidt's talent for the understatement and the indirect statement is already present. The military exploits of Goldschmidt's heroes have often been ridiculed, but Brøndsted has perceived that Goldschmidt himself treated them with a touch of irony.[8]

While *A Jew* possesses the flaws inevitable in a first novel, and is not as finished structurally as some of Goldschmidt's later works, it remains one of his most interesting and absorbing. Its immediate success was due largely to the novelty of the matter-of-fact depiction of the closed Jewish society, and this undoubtedly is one of the principal reasons for its continued popularity, but this does not entirely account for the interest with which the novel continues to be read. In spite of its exaggerations, the work is gripping in its sincerity; the reader, perhaps without being conscious of it, is being shown Goldschmidt's own feelings of bitterness and frustration. This quality, along with the historical interest presented by the picture of the culture within a culture, assures *A Jew* a permanent, secure place in Danish literature. Proof that the novel, unlike many "classics," continues to enjoy a wide reading public is given by the fact that it was reprinted as recently as 1968 in a popular, inexpensive paperback edition.

II Homeless

Homeless, Goldschmidt's second novel, is an impressive achievement—possibly too impressive, since its length (over nine hundred pages) has undoubtedly discouraged readers and made *Homeless* the least known of his novels. The novel's length and the fact that it was first published serially in Goldschmidt's periodical *Nord og Syd* (1853–1857) have influenced critics to pass judgment on the novel as rather formless, but in point of fact Goldschmidt constructed it according to a fixed plan. Goldschmidt had it published separately, apparently simultaneously with its appearance in *Nord og Syd* (some of the surviving volumes are labelled "second edition," but evidently constitute only a second printing, undertaken immediately after the first).

The novel resulted from Goldschmidt's European tour of 1846–1847. It represented the sum of Goldschmidt's experience and thinking up to that time, and is for that reason important to any study of Goldschmidt's development. Aside from the philosophical message which Goldschmidt was attempting to convey in the work, much of the narrative makes absorbing reading because of the detailed picture it presents of society and political states during the revolutionary years of the mid-nineteenth century. The philosophy behind *Homeless* is Gold-schmidt's evolving concept of Nemesis, which he here identifies with the Jewish "Shekinah," or God's mysterious presence in the world; Goldschmidt imparts to both concepts certain shades of meaning not ordinarily attached to them.

Literary historians and critics, influenced by Goldschmidt's own use—or overuse—of the word, tend almost invariably to employ the term "ideal" when describing the actions of the novel's hero; he is searching for the "ideal," he has betrayed the "ideal," he has found the "ideal" as he is dying, etc. Having said this, however, one has really said nothing, since the term possesses so many connotations that it is rendered almost meaningless. Like *A Jew*, *Homeless* is the story of a life (Goldschmidt gave the English version the subtitle *A Poet's Inner Life*). Also like *A Jew*, it is in three parts: "Hjemme" ("At Home"), "Hjemløs" ("Homeless"), and "Hjem" ("Homewards"), these terms to be understood in both real and symbolic meanings. Goldschmidt decided to make the hero of his second novel a Christian, in order to avoid the specific problems affecting the life of a Jew. Later, however, he regretted having done this, for in 1863 he wrote his family concerning a novel in English which he was writing (it was never finished), and he added that he was making up for the mistake in *Homeless*, in which the hero should have been a Jew.[9] There is, however, a Jewish element introduced into the novel quite early, in the form of a Sephardic family, the Mendozas (the hero of the unfinished English novel is also of Sephardic Jewish origin). The son and the daughter are about the same age as the hero, and the son, Alfons, plays an important part in the novel.

Otto Krøyer, the novel's central character, like Jacob Bendixen (and like Goldschmidt), grows up in a small provincial town where his father is a merchant. His two playmates are Emilie Theilmann, the daughter of a more prosperous merchant, and Peter Krøll, the son of a poor fisherman's widow. It is here that Otto is "at home," in harmony with himself, in his childhood world. His father owns a small trading ship, which he has named the *Marie Elisabeth* for his wife. The little vessel is the pride of the family and the symbol of their happiness and prosperity. When it is lost at sea, the misfortune is a sign that the family's prosperous days are over. Soon after, Otto's father is swindled in a commercial venture (mirroring an actual misfortune which befell Goldschmidt's father), and he becomes an embittered and broken man.

Otto's attachment to Emilie grows, and Otto's mother witnesses this with increasing displeasure and jealousy. She schemes to send Otto away to Copenhagen to attend school, in order to destroy the budding affection which threatens to take Otto away from her. Thereafter Otto sees Emilie only during school vacations, and is puzzled by her changing and unpredictable behavior as she, too, grows up.

In Copenhagen Otto lives with the erratic and somewhat exotic André family. The father, François, is a descendant of French émigrés, and the mother a Creole from the West Indies. The daughter is married to Hillebrandt, a house painter who had dreamed of being an artist; the son, Ferdinand, is a volatile, irresponsible personality. Carried away by Otto's highly romanticized descriptions of Emilie and his childhood home, Ferdinand falls in love with Emilie and goes to visit her and her family to ask for her hand. Emilie and her sisters make fun of him, and he returns to Copenhagen. When Otto learns of Ferdinand's unsuccessful courtship, it has the unexpected result of unleashing Otto's own love for Emilie, and he resolves to propose to her. In the meantime, Otto's father has died, and the barrier between Otto and his mother has grown. Otto returns home to court Emilie, but learns that she and the son of a local aristocrat have been seen flirting and kissing. This causes her to lose, in Otto's eyes, the poetic aura of purity, and with this last strong tie with his spiritual, childhood home broken, he returns to Copenhagen "homeless" in a real and a figurative sense.

Now a university student in Copenhagen, Otto is exposed to the inevitable erotic impulses. His reaction is to suspect his landlady of wishing to seduce him, and he moves into a hotel. His vague physical desires drive him out on the streets in the evening, and he wanders among the streetwalkers and prostitutes, without daring to respond to their advances. Finally, he is "rescued" from his feverish condition by visiting the Hillebrandts, where he learns that Mrs. Hillebrandt has recently given birth to a child and the act of holding the infant restores Otto's equilibrium.

The Jewish element reappears when Otto again meets Alfons Mendoza. Alfons, who is now studying music, helps Otto find a new "home," and the two immerse themselves in reading ancient writers and in attending the theater. A new friend of Otto's appears, a not too bright student nicknamed "Sem," the butt of jokes of the other students. At this point in Otto's development, he is introduced to Schiøtt (a portrait of Goldschmidt's mentor in aesthetics, P. L. Møller), and there follow lengthy student discussions of aesthetics, which constitute perhaps the least readable parts of the novel for the modern reader, but which are important in presenting Goldschmidt's own views on art and taste. Several other students participating in these discussions are also now introduced to the reader. At first glance, they seem to be unimportant to the course of the novel, but they will all reappear in roles of increasing importance as the work progresses. Among these are Helzen, Bregning, Hald, and Milner. After one of the student drinking parties, the drunken Sem mistakenly takes Otto's keys, so Otto must knock on his landlady's door to get to his room. Pauline, the landlady's seventeen-year-old daughter, answers the door, and while the two are talking, Pauline's mother appears, misunderstands the situation, and orders Otto to move out. The incident foreshadows Otto's future relationship with Pauline.

Schiøtt is the leader in all student discussions, whether on aesthetics, politics, or literature. His wide reading, and his keen and ironic mind make him easily the most adept of the group in intellectual debate. Otto soon looks up to him as his personal mentor (a reflection of Goldschmidt's earlier relationship to P. L. Møller).

Otto visits his mother and younger brother, who have been taken in by her sister and brother-in-law in a small country town. At first Otto impulsively wants to give up his studies and settle here to support his mother and brother, but soon the narrow-mindedness and generally limited quality of the small-town society is more than he can stand. He is rescued by an invitation from a local aristocrat, the father of one of Otto's student friends, to visit his estate. When he arrives the next day, he is told that his host is out with another guest, the "lady." Everyone is charmed by the "lady," and Otto learns that she is a certain famous actress from Copenhagen.

The actress, who is never named by Goldschmidt, completely captivates Otto and becomes a kind of false goddess for him (personal pronouns referring to her are capitalized), leading him away from the life and love he should have been seeking. Tormented and confused by his compulsive worship of her and by her reactions to his youthful advances, his erotic imagination is fired by his host's son's story of the conquest of a local miller's daughter, and Otto goes to the mill to attempt his own conquest. The attempt ends in a fiasco, however. On the way back from the mill, Otto meets a fourteen-year-old girl, who is to become the opposite pole to the actress in Otto's life. Symbolically, her name is Marie Elisabeth, the same as that of Otto's mother—and of his father's ship, that symbol of his childhood security and happiness. Otto is drawn to the girl, but is torn between his attractions for her and for the actress. The circle of Otto's life could have been closed already at this point, and he could have found happiness and personal fulfillment—a "home"—if only he could have recognized this fact. But he is too absorbed in his adoration of the actress.

Otto, having become acquainted with the life of the wealthy landed aristocracy, is now introduced to the aristocracy of blood, and—like Goldschmidt—he does not adapt well to the new society, and does not feel comfortable amid the new rules of social behavior. When the actress leaves the circle, it no longer has compelling interest for Otto.

Goldschmidt now begins to add to his gallery of portraits. Milner, until now presented only as an associate of Schiøtt's, is given a personality of his own. He is a minor civil servant, independently wealthy, without an original thought but with a great talent for appropriating the thoughts of others and passing them off as his own—in short, a promising young politician who is certain to make a name for himself. He decides to court Camilla Sander, the daughter of a wealthy businessman. Emilie Theilmann reappears, as a friend of Camilla's. The Theilmanns visit the Sanders, then go to a nearby resort. There a new face appears, a Dr. Dalberg, a prominent member of the opposition party, who tries to win Emilie's father for his party.

Milner persuades Schiøtt, from whom he has obtained most of his ideas, to come out to the resort, where Helzen, now a popular journalist with growing political power, and Hald join them; Bregning soon also reappears. Schiøtt is charmed by Emilie and decides to court her. In the end, however, neither Schiøtt nor Milner is successful; Emilie becomes engaged to Bregning, who is ordained a clergyman, and Camilla accepts Hald's proposal.

The formation of a political clique is now depicted, a picture taken from Goldschmidt's own experience. Of little interest to the modern reader, this segment of the novel was of great interest to Goldschmidt's contemporaries, who could recognize political figures of the day in some of the characters. The center of the clique is Dalberg, a portrait of the politician and writer Carl Ploug (1813–1894). Both Otto and Schiøtt are drawn into the group, and Schiøtt is eventually persuaded by Dalberg to write articles for the opposition party. The ensuing long discussions of political, aesthetic, and ethical questions offer little interest in themselves now, but they are valuable in that Goldschmidt's own views are presented in them. At one of the political "salons" Otto hears simultaneously of Emilie Theilmann's engagement and the actress's marriage. The young nobleman who announces the latter piece of news adds a slur on the reputation of the actress, and Otto flares up and insults the speaker. This act scandalizes the entire group and makes an implacable enemy of Milner, in whose home the scene took place.

Otto and Alfons resume their friendship, and in their conversations Mendoza tells something of his childhood, certain events of which actually happened to Goldschmidt himself. Otto witnesses Camilla's wedding to Hald, and is seized with a feeling of religiosity combined with a desire to be part of a family. At this point, he accidentally (although to Goldschmidt, nothing is really "accidental") meets Pauline, the daughter of his former landlady, and a love affair soon develops. Pauline's aunt, it turns out, is the widow of a man who had hanged himself after being swindled by Camilla's father, with the help of a lawyer named Basse—the same lawyer who had helped swindle

Otto's father (in Goldschmidt, it is indeed a small world). Pauline's aunt is Catholic, and this fact, too, is significant and points toward the future. Otto yearns for a genuine home and family life, and decides to ask officially for Pauline's hand, to which Pauline's parents readily agree. But Otto's intellectually aristocratic nature will not conform to the narrow world of Pauline's parents, and the engagement is soon broken off, and Otto and Pauline return to their clandestine affair.

The action involving all the characters increases in tempo. Alfons plays before the king and is such a success that the king offers him a stipend to travel and study abroad. Camilla's and Hald's marriage has not been happy; their first child dies, and Camilla's father interprets this as punishment for his having swindled Pauline's uncle ("Nemesis"). Otto and Pauline break off their relationship, and Otto later learns that Ferdinand André has become engaged to her, since she has inherited a sizeable amount of money from the aunt. Otto has written a play, which is successful when it is first staged, but subsequently is attacked by a conspiracy of Otto's political enemies who control the newspapers, and Otto withdraws it. The actress and her husband, a titled aristocrat, turn up in the opposition political camp. Disillusioned, Otto begins to frequent the company of some hard-drinking young officers.

Camilla Hald has now taken her place as a leading society woman, since her father has died and left the Halds his fortune. But she is no longer happy with the shallow and limited Hald, and is intrigued with Otto's conversation when they meet in society.

Schiøtt now seems to be part of the enemy camp, and Otto's only friend is apparently Alfons. Otto is ready for another drastic change. At this point he "accidentally" meets Peter Krøll again. Krøll plans to go abroad, and shows signs of developing into an inventor. Schiøtt is now the literary critic for an influential newspaper, and has acquired power and influence himself. During the conversation with Otto, he suggests that Otto write his ideas down in the form of letters, and Schiøtt will have them printed. In order to conceal his own connection with Otto, since this would damage his position with the political party, Schiøtt enlists Sem as a go-between. When the letters are published, Helzen and Milner, intent on discovering the author, since the letters are hostile to their party's interests, trick Sem into disclosing Schiøtt's connection. In order to destroy Schiøtt, their unquestioned intellectual superior, Milner, Helzen, and Hald stage a satirical comedy holding Schiøtt up to ridicule (the same thing had actually happened to Goldschmidt). Otto challenges Helzen to a duel, but the latter refuses, and the young aristocratic officer whom Otto has chosen as his second is banished abroad by his relatives.

Alfons is to go to Italy to study, and Otto and Schiøtt take part in a farewell party for him. Otto suddenly notices that Schiøtt has no shirt on under his coat. Schiøtt has been completely ruined by the political clique, who have seen to it that he has lost his position with the newspaper, and his creditors have descended on him. As Otto and Schiøtt are riding away from the party, Schiøtt is knocked from his horse by a passing carriage and seriously injured. By "chance" (Nemesis) the passenger in the carriage is Schiøtt's first youthful love. She recognizes him and takes him to her estate to have his injuries treated. There Otto takes leave of him, to go abroad himself.

The rest of the second part of the novel is crammed with Otto's travel experiences in Italy and Switzerland, paralleling Goldschmidt's own. The reader of Goldschmidt's own time might have been fatigued by the detailed travel descriptions, but to the modern reader, conscious of Goldschmidt's own travels in 1846–1847, this section is among the most interesting of the whole work.

Since there are no chance meetings or coincidences—every encounter is either a direct cause or a direct effect—when the attentive reader learns that the Halds are also going to Italy and that the actress and her husband are already there, he realizes that Otto will soon meet them all. On the stagecoach to Prague Otto has already met a pair of exiled Italian noblewomen—sisters—and it is inevitable that Otto will meet them again, too. In Rome, Otto is soon an "accidental" eavesdropper on a quarrel between the actress on the one hand and her husband and his mother on the other. Still unaccustomed to the distinguished social circles she now moves in, she has committed some social error and is being strongly criticized by her husband

and mother-in-law. Finally she fights back, threatening to return
to the theater, and at this the others crumble and apologize.
Left alone, as she thinks, since she is unaware of Otto's presence,
she muses over what Otto takes to be their first acquaintance
and his love for her. She later realizes that he has been eavesdropping, and has her revenge.

When Otto and Alfons again meet, in Rome, Otto finds that
the devout Jew has been affected by the pervasive Catholicism
of Italy, just as Goldschmidt himself was. Alfons has made the
acquaintance of several monks in a monastery, and through him
Otto is introduced to some of them, including the calculating
Father Benedict, two Jesuit monks, and the strange fanatic Fra
Jacobeo, who was born of Jewish parents in India, was taken
to England and baptized by an English clergyman, but, dis-
satisfied with Protestantism, became a Catholic and came to
Rome. The Catholic monks are bent on converting Otto, and
the arguments they use, given at length by Goldschmidt, probably reflect discussions which Goldschmidt had had in Rome
when he was toying with Catholicism. In the meantime, Otto
has begun an affair with his Italian landlady, who, on instruc-
tions from her confessor, is also eagerly trying to convert him.

When Carnival begins, Otto is at first reluctant to take part,
but he eventually surrenders to the mood and goes out on the
streets to be a part of the mass celebrations. He meets Alfons,
and the latter, who had been on the point of converting to
Catholicism, has just witnessed the yearly ceremony in which
Jews from the ghetto were forced to kneel and beg for permission to live there the coming year, as well as to pay the costs
of the Roman horse races. As a result, Alfons bitterly turns away
from Catholicism. In the spirit of the Carnival celebrations,
Otto throws a flower to a veiled woman in a carriage. The
experienced Goldschmidt reader realizes that chance plays no
role here, and that Otto will later meet and recognize this
mysterious woman.

Alfons has visited an Italian music professor (a Christian)
and the man's daughter has fallen in love with Alfons. Since
her love is unrequited, she has become a nun. Otto is poetically
enchanted with the idea of unreturned love causing a girl to

renounce the world and enter a convent (this, too, foreshadows Otto's future).

Otto and Alfons become acquainted with Sir James Mocatta (a portrait of Sir Moses Montefiore, the English Jewish philanthropist) and his family, including his nephew de Castro (named for a friend of Montefiore's). The ensuing philosophical conversations between Otto and de Castro form a stage for airing Goldschmidt's budding idea of Nemesis.

Otto again meets the woman to whom he had thrown the flower, and it is no surprise to the reader to learn that she is none other than Camilla Hald. Otto learns that the Halds are now going to Switzerland.

De Castro leads in the destruction of the wall surrounding the ghetto (the event actually took place a year earlier than Goldschmidt describes it). The fanatic monk Fra Jacobeo takes part in the event and is suddenly overcome by his awareness of his kinship with the Jews of the ghetto, and curses the Catholic mob. He is shot by someone in the mob, and attains the martyrdom he had longed for. Father Benedict appears, denies Jacobeo's fall from Catholicism, and offers a reward for the "Protestant" or "Englishman" who killed him. Later, the actress overhears Otto and Alfons discussing the event and in an unclear desire for revenge for Otto's earlier eavesdropping, she casts suspicion on him. His jealous and disappointed landlady leads the angry mob to his room, but at the last minute saves his life, and he escapes with Alfons and de Castro to Genoa, then to Geneva.

In Geneva, Otto almost immediately "accidentally" meets the two exiled Italian noblewomen whom he had earlier met on his travels. He also by "chance" meets the Halds again. The revolution of 1848 has broken out in France, and all are seized by the universal unrest. Inspired by Camilla's suggestion that Denmark's sons should stand by Denmark rather than join other nations' great movements, Otto suddenly decides to return home. By this time he is in love with both the Italian countess and Camilla Hald.

In an inn in an alpine village, Otto has another "chance" encounter. A sick foreigner there turns out to be Peter Krøll, who had left Denmark to search for freedom and a rich patron

to support his mechanical invention, and has ended by falling
ill of malnutrition and exposure here in the Alps. Otto returns
to Geneva with him and introduces him to de Castro, who
will finance Peter's work on his invention. From Geneva Otto
goes to join the Halds in the Swiss town where Hald is recover-
ing from a fall in the mountains. Predictably, the bond between
Otto and Camilla grows stronger.

In a small town nearby, Otto comes upon a cloister and is
struck by the voice of one of the nuns as they are singing inside.
Otto and Camilla arrange to meet at the cloister to decide their
future together. The nun who comes out to escort them in the
cloister—the same nun whose singing so charmed Otto—proves
to be none other than Pauline, Otto's betrayed mistress and the
niece of the man Camilla's father had ruined (double Nemesis).
When Camilla learns of Otto's role in Pauline's past, she can
no longer think of a life together with him. At this moment
Camilla realizes she is pregnant with Hald's child (Nemesis
again). Pauline's fate is also sealed, for the father confessor of
the convent says that almost all of the nuns sent here die within
five years (Nemesis settling accounts with her, too). Goldschmidt
has thus tidied up the fates of several of his leading characters.
A short time before the debacle, Otto had defined his (and
Goldschmidt's) Nemesis concept: "Every misfortune stems from
an error, and every good fortune stems from a good deed." In
the triangle Camilla-Otto-Pauline, they are all three guilty of
an "error," and Goldschmidt's divine balance can be restored
only by all three accepting their "punishment."

Otto now returns to Italy, determined to take part in the
world's great events as revolutions spread. He meets the Italian
countesses again, and through them, a mercenary republican
general and his fellow officer, a colonel. Otto joins the general's
command, and learns that there is bad blood between the two
officers. The general is obsessed by the thought that he earlier
killed his wife and their unborn child, and will be punished for
it (Nemesis). The following section of the narrative, dealing
with the military activity around Otto, in some of which he
participates, is undoubtedly a weak point in the novel, but Goldschmidt had an addiction for describing military life as he saw
it. Otto and the Italian countess, their cause apparently betrayed,

make their way to Paris, and on the way Otto is forced to witness the general's rigged and impromptu court martial and execution for betrayal; the general had foretold his own death, and attributed it to his having caused the death of his unborn child, but as Otto predicts, the general will now in turn cause the death of his murderers (Nemesis once again). Disillusioned and embittered, Otto decides to return to Denmark, and proposes marriage to the countess, but she refuses and he must leave alone.

The concluding part of the novel, entitled "Homeward," depicts Otto's return to Denmark, his worldly home, then his ultimate spiritual return to the "home" of his childhood—to the peace, secure self-harmony, and truth he had not known since childhood. To his mother's question as to what he has become as a result of his travels, Otto answers, as Goldschmidt had said about himself after his own travels, "I think I have become more of a human being."

All the old threads are brought together, and a few new ones are spun and united. Alfons has married the Mocattas' daughter, and his father-in-law has bought an estate for him. But Alfons' music has been rejected by Danish critics, as "unnational" (an accusation with which Goldschmidt was personally familiar), and he wants to leave Denmark. Alfons' sister is married and has a son, who has been named for Otto. Schiøtt is now married to his first love, the same woman who had run him down in her carriage. Schiøtt has given up the idealism of his youth in favor of power and influence. He has employed Sem as a sort of valet.

The political opportunists, Otto's former enemies, have all succeeded in attaining posts, influence, and fame. The actress is now a respected and powerful figure in their party. At one of their social events, she breaks with Otto for good, and the political party once again uses its power against him, so that he is left virtually friendless and alone. One of the local noblemen proposes a diplomatic post for him, and as the first step toward this new career, Otto must be elected a member of the parliament.

Otto is now again drawn to Marie Elisabeth, but she is repulsed by his obvious infatuation with Emilie and becomes engaged to one of Otto's former student friends. Otto and Emilie

arrange a tryst when her husband is away, and she contrives
to leave her window open, but her husband returns unexpectedly, before Otto arrives, so nothing comes of the plan. Nemesis
has had a hand in frustrating both of Otto's erotic plans—he
wanted to marry Marie Elisabeth only for selfish reasons, to have
a nice, acceptable little wife; and his attempted seduction of
Emilie would have been a transgression against real love, since
it could have led nowhere. Returning from his thwarted seduction attempt, Otto sees that Marie Elisabeth's house is on fire.
He rescues everyone from the blazing house, but is injured in
the act. After the fire, Otto realizes that his real mission in
life is to be a teacher for the workers in the factory which
Peter Krøll is building in the neighborhood, financed by de
Castro. All thoughts of a diplomatic career are given up. Otto's
injury, however, proves to be fatal, and Otto is reconciled to
dying, having at last found his way "home," and as he dies, in
the presence of his mother, Emilie, and Marie Elisabeth, he
has a symbolic vision of himself as a child, the family's ship the
Marie Elisabeth (all three "Marie Elisabeths" are brought together), and his father.

There are so many threads in *Homeless* that it is easy to parody
the novel and to emphasize its seeming formlessness. Goldschmidt's central idea was present from first to last, however.
He was obsessed with the idea of demonstrating his philosophy
of Nemesis—one cause and one effect, crime and punishment,
the continual readjustment of the divine balance in worldly
existence; he intended to show this divine balancing in the life
of one individual. If the reader forgets that for Goldschmidt
there are no coincidences, no chance occurrences, and no acci-
dents, then the novel becomes hardly more than one long series
of sometimes wildly improbable accidental encounters. But if
one enters into an understanding with Goldschmidt and accepts
the author's belief in the presence of cause and effect in even
the smallest occurrences in life, the work acquires a unity which
has been denied it by some critics. Any literary work may be
easily parodied, especially by a critic such as Georg Brandes,
and once it has been subjected to parody, a later critic finds it
difficult to view the work seriously. Otto's death at the end of
Homeless, for example, has been subjected to such a treatment,

but in an extremely condensed form—a little over two pages—
Goldschmidt's description of Otto's acceptance of imminent
death need not fear comparison with Tolstoy's world-famous
story on this subject, *The Death of Ivan Ilyich*, which was not
published until 1886.

Homeless was translated into German almost simultaneously
with its publication in Danish (1854–1858). The English version, *Homeless, or a Poet's Inner Life*, is more than a translation.
It was extensively revised by Goldschmidt, who was by this
time writing in English, and is characterized by a general
tightening of the structure. In every respect except the language
(the Victorian English is dated, while Goldschmidt's Danish
has not aged in a negative sense), the English version is superior
to the Danish *Homeless*. Originally, *Homeless* was to have been
translated by Mrs. Howitt, one of the translators of *A Jew*. A
note in *Nord og Syd*, in English, states, "Mrs. Howitt is authorized to translate this work into English and receives it in
manuscript from the author."[10] It is not known what changed
Goldschmidt's plans, but in view of Mrs. Howitt's demonstrated
incompetence as a translator of Danish, it is well that she was
not entrusted with the work. Later, Goldschmidt wanted to
commission Frederica Maclean Rowan (1814–1882) to do the
translation. She was a competent linguist—her mother was from
Bergen, Norway, and Frederica had lived in Copenhagen. She
knew four languages and was a noted translator from French
and German. She was a secretary to Sir Francis Goldsmid
(1808–1878)—a well-known lawyer and political figure, the first
Jew to become an English barrister, whom Goldschmidt also
knew very well in London. Judging from Goldschmidt's correspondence of the time, Miss Rowan was to be paid by Benjamin
Rothschild. It is not clear what happened between Goldschmidt
and Miss Rowan, but she evidently did not proceed with the
translation. Her name is not mentioned anywhere in the English
version of the novel, although her name appears prominently on
translations known to have been made by her. Goldschmidt
mentions, in several of his letters of that period, that he was
making his own revisions in English, and there is ample proof
that his English at that time was indeed good enough to enable
him to do this. Hester Rothschild assisted him as the final editor

of the English, and Goldschmidt thanks her for this in a dedication. This in no way negates his being given credit for revising his own work, since it is common practice among multilingual writers and scholars to have their work in a language not native to them edited by a native speaker of that language. On the strength of all available evidence, therefore, Goldschmidt may be given full credit for revising the work in English. *Homeless, or a Poet's Inner Life*, then, assumes an importance greater than that of a mere translation—it becomes, in effect, an original work and should be evaluated on that basis.

In a preface to the English version, lacking in the original, Goldschmidt states his purpose in writing the novel: "... in truth, that which is commonly called the reality of life is not my work's chief object and aim. Above that reality which we see and hear of, there is yet another reality—life's true pith, the true goal of existence, which minds of noble stamp dimly see from early youth, though mingled with and obscured by their passions; and for which they strive, but, alas! often as a vessel without compass, surrounded by fogs. This reality is the ideal." Whatever Goldschmidt critics have meant at various times by the "ideal," Goldschmidt's own words give an indication of what he himself meant by the term.

III   The Heir

Structurally, Goldschmidt's third novel, *The Heir*, is superior to *Homeless*, if not to the more economically constructed English version, *Homeless, or a Poet's Inner Life*. *The Heir* is a parallel to *Homeless*, but contains fewer threads, fewer important characters, and no Jewish elements—all of which, while making *Homeless* cumbersome, give it the depth and life which are somehow lacking in *The Heir*. As a novel of ideas, *The Heir* is inferior to *Homeless*. It was first published in 1865, as the third and final volume of *Fortællinger og Skildringer* (*Stories and Descriptions*), and appeared separately the following year. Like *Homeless*, *The Heir* has two principal themes—Nemesis and a hero in search of his true mission in life. Unlike Otto Krøyer, however, Axel, the hero of *The Heir*, presumably lives to carry out his mission. But like Otto, Axel is prevented by Nemesis from being united with his life's true love. In contrast to *Homeless, The Heir* is told in the first person; what is gained in immediacy by this device is lost in breadth of viewpoint.

Axel, the central character in *The Heir*, is the son of a wealthy landowner, and almost from birth he is made aware of the fact that he is the heir to the estate, and that he has a responsibility to it and to its tenants. Besides Axel's family—his parents and a younger sister—the household includes a retired cavalry officer, an old friend of Axel's father. When Axel is about ten years old, he is sent for schooling to a neighboring manor, where the landowner keeps a teacher for his five sons, the youngest of whom, Valdemar, becomes Axel's lifelong friend (as well as brother-in-law). Later, after his mother's death, Axel is sent to Copenhagen for further schooling.

Among Axel's acquaintances in Copenhagen is a Dr. Hilder, whose niece Sophie is one of Axel's playmates in the garden of the house of the customs official with whom Axel lives. In the neighboring garden Axel sees a little girl, Astrid, with whom he falls in love for life. Meanwhile, Axel's father is swindled out of a large sum of money (like Otto's father in *Homeless*, and like Goldschmidt's father), and the estate is taken away from him by the court. This catastrophe eventually causes the deaths of both Axel's father and his friend, the retired cavalry officer.

Axel, now in greatly reduced circumstances, must attend a less expensive school and live in more modest quarters. He moves into the home of a horse trader with whom the cavalry officer had dealt. Dr. Hilder tactfully rescues Axel from this situation and invites him to move into his apartment, which he shares with Sophie and her mother. Axel finishes school, enters the university, and dreams of becoming an army officer. Valdemar attends the naval academy, becomes a naval officer, and falls in love with Axel's sister. Axel continues to love Astrid (whose name begins to appear in spaced type, the equivalent of italics; later, pronouns referring to Astrid are capitalized, as was the case of the actress in *Homeless*), but has no opportunity to declare himself.

For a time, Axel is obsessed by a compulsion to gamble. Once, when the stakes are high, he is tempted to cheat, and although he resists the temptation, he feels that he has betrayed his father, the principles of the cavalry officer, and his love for Astrid, and vows never to gamble again. Later, while he is observing a card game without participating in it, he is approached by a count from Holstein, who is impressed by Axel's refusal to gamble and asks Axel to be his son's traveling companion on the latter's grand tour through Europe. The son is a compulsive gambler, and the father hopes that Axel will be able to counteract the young man's mania. At this time, Axel learns from the count that one of the count's relatives, a Swedish nobleman, has become engaged to Astrid. The Swede, Baron Panin, has been twice married, and Axel further learns that the only reason Astrid has agreed to marry him is that her sister has just died, leaving her twin children orphaned, and the Baron has agreed to adopt them. Crushed by the news, Axel goes to visit Dr. Hilder. Sophie is there alone, and when she tries to comfort him, both are overcome with passion, with the inevitable result. Now both Axel and Astrid have "sinned" against their true love, and the reader has only to wait for Nemesis to begin redressing the balance.

Dr. Hilder learns of the affair, and while not blaming Axel, he insists on a *pro forma* marriage with an immediate divorce, to protect Sophie's reputation. It is tempting to see in the seduction and meaningless marriage a telescoped and romanticized version of Goldschmidt's own affair with Johanne Sonne. As a sort of mirror image of Axel's affair, Valdemar comes in all good form to ask for the hand of Axel's sister. With no bonds any longer tying him, Axel agrees to accompany the count's son on his European tour.

The tour proves to consist largely of visits to gambling casinos. In a German casino Axel and the young count meet another young gambler, de Potter, the son of a Belgian banker. Axel soon comes to feel that he is wasting his talents, and attends lectures at the local university. Eventually the two young men arrive in Paris, where they renew their acquaintance with de Potter, and the latter and the young count engage in a continuing duel at the gaming tables. In conversations with de Potter, Axel realizes that de Potter has human qualities which could redeem him, if he could overcome his insane compulsion for gambling. They feel drawn to each other, but de Potter is unable to combat his mania. Finally, at the conclusion of a game in which he has lost to the young count, de Potter shoots himself while still sitting at the table. The young count collapses in shock, and upon recovery swears never to gamble again. In Vienna, where they go next, Axel, on an errand for the count, goes into a bank. There one of the directors turns out to be de Potter's uncle (Nemesis at work). The young de Potter had written to his family about his conversations with Axel, and the uncle is favorably disposed toward Axel, who is introduced into the uncle's social circle, which includes a high Viennese police official, von Hradziwick.

Meanwhile, Axel feels that the friendship between him and the young count has grown cold, as a result of the de Potter affair, and they both look for a chance to break it off. Axel hits upon an undisclosed field of research, asks one of his new acquaintances about publishing his work, and is referred to a private library in Italy which contains a unique collection in just this field; Axel is given permission to use the collection. The young count's father has meanwhile arrived in Vienna to take charge of his son, so Axel departs for Italy.

The library is in a castle, and Axel receives an official order from the Austrian authorities governing the area to take complete charge of the library. In the general unrest it is expected that the local insurgents will attempt to sack the castle and destroy its library and museum. At this point Axel receives a letter from home notifying him that his ancestral manor has been willed back to him by the repentant man who had swindled his father (Nemesis). When the castle is attacked, Axel has organized the few Austrian soldiers under his command so well that he repulses the attackers and saves the castle and its contents. As a result, he is made an officer and decorated.

Before returning to Denmark to take over his estate, Axel decides to travel in Italy and the Near East. His sister and Valdemar, who have taken charge of the estate for him, are to join him. Rome is his first major destination; it is not the Rome of *Homeless*, that of Goldschmidt's tour of 1847, but that of his visit in 1863. Goldschmidt's attitude toward the city is still one of enthusiasm, but critical notes now creep in—for example

Axel/Goldschmidt takes a swipe at the self-isolating Scandinavian artists' colony in Rome, a circle which Goldschmidt came to know intimately during his stay in Rome in 1863.

At a soiree at the home of an American family, Axel suddenly comes face to face with Astrid (another of the many noncoincidences in Goldschmidt). His renewed love for Astrid and their constantly being together probably represent a romanticization of Goldschmidt's own infatuation with Mrs. Stilling in 1863. Astrid's sister's children are then a reflex of Mrs. Stilling's own children.

The old count from Holstein and his family now turn up in Rome. The parents have taken the young count on a tour to attempt to restore his mental health after the shock of de Potter's violent suicide, but nothing has helped; the young man, while adhering to his vow never to gamble again, has not found any substitute for his gambling passion, and has sunk into apathy and indifference. The old count is surprised to find that Axel is now his equal, since Axel has recovered his estate. The old count stresses that he will spare no means whatever to restore his son's interest in life; this declaration prepares the reader for sinister events to come. The young count resents Axel, since the latter reminds him of de Potter and since he now has no control over Axel.

When the young count suddenly shows a renewed interest in life when he is in Astrid's presence, and the old count repeats his assertion that he will spare nothing and no one for the sake of his son, the cloud of impending catastrophe becomes thicker, and when the count says that he has found the right medicine for his son, Axel dimly fears the worst. The young count publicly insults Axel, who dons his uniform and awaits satisfaction. The old count intervenes, however, and hustles his son off to Vienna on a mysterious errand, leaving his wife behind to attend Astrid. The mystery deepens when Astrid's husband, the Swedish baron, also appears in Vienna. It becomes even murkier when Astrid receives orders from her husband to leave Rome for Naples.

Through another Goldschmidt noncoincidence, Axel unexpectedly encounters Salling, the horse trader with whom he had lived in Copenhagen while attending school. Salling is now a coachman for Baron Panin, Astrid's husband, who has come to Rome with an Italian princess with the avowed intention of marrying her. Axel now fears for Astrid, and hurries to Naples, only to learn that she has been taken to Vienna. Axel immediately dashes off to Vienna, where he manages to locate Astrid by disguising himself as a servant, but he is arrested as a spy. Fortunately (another noncoincidence), he is taken for interrogation to his old friend, von Hradziwick, to whom Axel explains the situation. The police official promises Axel his aid. Later, Axel sees and overhears Salling and the young count planning what is obviously an abduction, and Axel appeals to von Hradziwick for help. Von Hradziwick gives him a blanket arrest order, and adds a secret symbol to insure close guard of the person arrested. Axel succeeds dramatically in thwarting the abduction plot, which of course had Astrid as its object. At the instant when the young count springs onto Astrid's carriage to carry out the abduction, which was to take place in front of an inn, the woman of the inn calls out the name "de Potter," and the shock to the young count is so great that he falls down in an epileptic fit (the name of the innkeeper is Depotter—Nemesis at its most clear-cut).

Although Axel has thus rescued Astrid, he later learns that the Swedish baron has officially divorced Astrid and has by force sent her away, but for revenge has taken the two children and is on his way to Salzburg to have them placed in a cloister to be brought up Catholic. Axel pursues him, overtakes him and frees the children, and by using the secret arrest order he has the baron sent under guard back to Vienna. Axel takes the children and hurries to Geneva, where he immediately catches sight of Astrid and his sister, who has come with Valdemar to join Axel. Axel and Astrid are at last betrothed to each other, but she requires time to recover from her recent harrowing experiences before they can be married. The party goes to Naples, but they are there overtaken by Baron Panin and his party. Axel and his little group are rescued by an English naval captain and taken on board his ship. He conveys them to Syria, which they had planned to visit before returning to Denmark. Astrid's exhausted condition worsens, and when they reach a place significantly named Ehden, she dies, but not before she and Axel experience the meaning of true love. Nemesis has settled accounts with her—since she prostituted herself in the marriage with Baron Panin. Although her motives were not selfish, she had betrayed the "ideal" of true love and thus had no right to true love in this world. Nemesis' hand has also punished Axel for his transgression with Sophie, of course.

Axel is now left with the firm resolve to return to his estate, build it up, and become a force for social improvement, a resolve Astrid had instilled in him with her ideas concerning the social responsibilities of the wealthy and aristocratic. He is thus her spiritual heir, as well as the actual heir to his father's estate. The children will in turn inherit all his good works. The real meaning of the novel's title lies in his acceptance of the social responsibility of the wealthy class toward the masses, which Astrid has evolved as a member of that class, and has now bequeathed to him.

In a sense, *The Heir* is a simplified *Homeless*, shorn of many of the variations in character and many of the travel descriptions, which may have been somewhat tedious to Goldschmidt's contemporaries, but which amply repay the modern reader's efforts. In *The Heir* Goldschmidt has deliberately focussed narrowly on his two major themes—the action of Nemesis in the lives of all and the search of a talented individual for self-realization. Goldschmidt was a brilliant conversationalist himself, and was adept at depicting sustained intellectual conversation—a talent which he did not use nearly so much in *The Heir* as he had in *Homeless*. Although *The Heir* has recently (1969) been reprinted in a popular paperback series, as a lasting significant literary accomplishment it seems to stand well below *Homeless*, which has not been reprinted since 1919.

The Heir has apparently not been translated into other languages. Although the British journal *The Athenæum* announced (in its number of 31 December 1864) that the novel was being translated into English, the translation evidently was never completed. Bibliographically misleading is the listing for the translation, for example, in the British Museum catalog entry for *The Heir;* the citation, in fact, is for a seven-page brochure containing a translation of excerpts of the first chapter, and the last chapter.[11]

IV The Raven

Goldschmidt's fourth and last full-length novel, *The Raven*, is technically probably his best, although it lacks the interest presented by the realistic portrayals of society in *A Jew* and *Homeless*. It is, as Mogens Brøndsted has called it, a modern fairy tale, combining the fantastic with the realistic. The plot is simple, and the conclusion—given Goldschmidt's preoccupation with his peculiar vision of Nemesis—is inevitable. The story's framework is built around the familiar Goldschmidt theme of a ship's insurance swindle and the resultant ruin of a formerly prosperous upper-class family, with the eventual unmasking and punishment of the villain, and the victim's descendants being restored to their rights. The story unfolds gradually; at first the victim's descendants do not even fully realize that the grandfather was cheated, and only toward the end do they find out who the villain was. The villain is introduced first, and there is not one, but the folkloristic three, "heroes," the grandsons of the original victim. This represents a radical departure from Goldschmidt's usual single central figure.

Again, the novel is in three parts. The first introduces a mysterious man of wealth, apparently from the New World, who is eager to be accepted by Copenhagen's high society, and three working-class brothers, whose half-mad grandmother once belonged to the wealthier class. The wealthy newcomer, Abraham Krog, has engaged a Jewish agent to carry out small commissions and confidential errands. This Jew, Simon Levi, is Goldschmidt's most memorable characterization, and the lasting fame of the novel rests primarily on the beautifully alive, psychologically perfectly constructed figure of the little hunchbacked Jew.

Of the three Carøe brothers, the middle one, Ferdinand, appears first, and while not the most intelligent of the brothers, he is the most engaging. He is ship's boy on a small naval vessel commanded by Captain Winter (a stimulus for the novel was a visit Goldschmidt had made on board a naval vessel). On a visit to his aunt, Ferdinand tells his grandmother, who has a reputation for being a prophetess, of reading in one of his captain's books about a raven from Iceland which has in its beak a stone that will enable its finder to have three wishes

fulfilled.[12] The grandmother's ambiguous response seems to con-
firm the raven's existence, and Ferdinand determines to find the
raven, and with the three wishes for him and his two brothers,
to restore the fortunes of his family.

There has been a theft of the captain's money, and Ferdinand
is suspected, but Ferdinand and his superstitious relatives, in
a sort of spiritualistic session, determine that the guilty person
is the cook. Later, the cook, who has injured his eye apparently
as a result of the mysterious intervention of Ferdinand's grandmother, confesses to Ferdinand, and the money is returned, but
Ferdinand is still under suspicion. These apparently minor events
exercise an influence on later events, as is to be expected in
Goldschmidt's Nemesis-dominated world.

The youngest Carøe brother, Morten, who possesses mechanical talent, was modeled on Goldschmidt's own brother Moritz,
who himself established a textile factory. The oldest of the
brothers, Vilhelm, is the intellectual, for whom the others,
especially the mother, must work and sacrifice in order to enable
him to become a medical student at the university. Vilhelm visits
Ferdinand on the ship, and meets Ottilie, a cousin of Captain
Winter. She is the daughter of a wealthy retired officer, and thus
a member of the upper class, and beyond the reach of Vilhelm,
although an attachment develops between them.

Two satellite figures appear in Krog's growing circle—the
functionary Ask and the would-be poet Ibald. Ibald writes a
flattering poem dedicated to Krog, which, when published, has
far-reaching effects on the Krog family. Becker, a celebrated
actor who lives across from the Krogs, decides to court the
oldest Krog daughter Ellinor, and uses the poem as an excuse
to become acquainted with the Krogs. Courtship and marriage
follow.

Krog, apparently salving his conscience for some past mis-
deed, establishes a fund for a Seilstrup family which Simon
Levi has located, but this turns out to be the wrong family.
Ferdinand's grandmother is named Seilstrup, and eventually
Krog "accidentally" sees her. There is mutual recognition, and
she dies of the shock.

During the war over Schleswig-Holstein, both Ferdinand and
Vilhelm distinguish themselves, and Vilhelm is promoted to the

rank of an officer. Morten Carøe, on his way home from Flens-
burg, where he was serving his apprenticeship, is arrested as
a spy and brought to Ottilie's father, who is back on active duty.
He is convinced of Morten's innocence, and eventually helps him
build a factory based on one of his inventions (for a similar
characterization, see Peter Krøll in *Homeless*). In order to get
more capital, Krog, who is a neighbor of Ottilie Winter and her
father, is brought into the enterprise, and he soon has control
of the undertaking and plots to oust the Carøes from it entirely.
In the meantime, Krog decides to launch himself upon a political
career. In exchange for Simon Levi's help, Krog promises to
have Levi appointed a lottery collector, a post which has long
been the object of Levi's dreams. But Krog finds it politically
expedient to recommend a more influential man for the position,
and thus makes a bitter, though secret, enemy of Levi.

During this period, Ellinor's marriage with Becker is disinte-
grating because of Becker's completely egocentric behavior.
Hansen, an officer whose life Vilhelm saved in the war, is in
love with Ellinor, but convinced of the hopelessness of his love,
he resolves to emigrate. Vilhelm, still in love with Ottilie but
separated from her by class differences, devotes his time to social
work among the factory personnel (see Otto Krøyer in *Homeless*),
some of whom he recognizes as his old comrades in arms.
Jeremy, Krog's son, whom his father wants to marry Ottilie, falls
in love instead with a serving girl in Becker's house.

Meanwhile, Ferdinand has sailed to South America on the
presumed trail of the luck-bringing raven. In one of Goldschmidt's noncoincidences, he overhears a passenger describing
a case of embezzlement resembling the swindling of his grandfather, certain vague details of which the brothers have learned
from some old letters and papers found after their grandmother's
death. Later, in another nonaccident, Ferdinand saves the passenger's life, and when they become acquainted, the man gives
Ferdinand an old letter from the embezzler, written from Chicago and signed by the name of Krog. Ferdinand determines
to go to Chicago to try to find Krog.

Ottilie and her father visit the Carøes' factory, where the
brothers are planning to emigrate with their mother and Hansen,
since Krog has deprived them of control of the factory. Ottilie

gradually loses her haughty class consciousness and comes to esteem Vilhelm's mother. Simon Levi is sent to the factory to inventory some of the goods, and he arrives at the same time as Ferdinand, who is returning from the United States without having found either the raven or the embezzler. The man whose life Ferdinand had saved in South America was a friend of Simon Levi's years before (one of Goldschmidt's noncoincidences), and Levi had lent him money to leave Denmark. Now the man has given Ferdinand a gold coin to give to Levi, if he "chances" to find Levi. Ibald, who has accompanied Levi to the factory, as a practical joke persuades Levi to ride a donkey. The animal pitches Levi off and Ferdinand, who "happens" to be standing there, catches him in midair, saving him from serious injury. When identities are established, Ferdinand gives Levi the gold coin and tells him of his adventures in South America and his quest in the United States for "Krog." When Levi sees the signature on the old letter from Chicago, he recognizes his employer's handwriting, and renounces his loyalty to Krog—a business loyalty that had endured in spite of Levi's personal enmity to Krog—and shows that the man who ruined Ferdinand's grandfather is none other than the wealthy and powerful Krog. The brothers take the proof to a lawyer, then go to confront Krog, who is now a titular councillor of state and a member of parliament. He is at that moment giving a dinner for his party leaders, who are proposing Krog for a high political position. The sudden appearance of the brothers, and Ferdinand's crying out Krog's real name stun the man, and he signs the factory over to them. Krog now gives up all his political ambitions and emigrates with his family. His second daughter will get the bridegroom she loves, the son will get to marry the serving girl, and Hansen, the officer in love with Ellinor (who is now divorced from Becker) "happens" to be sailing on the same ship with the Krogs. Ottilie realizes that the Carøes are true aristocrats in that they are working for others, and now realizes that she has always loved Vilhelm, whom she now accepts as her bridegroom with his mother's blessing.

The Raven has enjoyed continuing popularity in Denmark; it has been reprinted several times, most recently in 1971. It occupies an assured place among Danish classic novels, primarily because of Goldschmidt's flawless prose style, which reaches its peak here, and because of Goldschmidt's masterpiece of characterization, Simon Levi. The novel has not been translated into English, but it has appeared in German—a German translation was published as early as 1886.

Of his two recurrent themes—Nemesis and the individual's search for self-harmony and a mission in life—only Nemesis remains in clear-cut form in *The Raven*. Vilhelm's interest in social improvement and profit sharing does not become a central theme, although the presence of the social ideas does attest Goldschmidt's lifelong interest in the improvement of working and living conditions of the so-called working classes.

Although Goldschmidt is commonly thought of as producing his best work in short stories and novellas, it was as a novelist that he first became known in imaginative literature. *A Jew* is still in many ways his most interesting work, and it deserves to be reintroduced to English readers in a more competent translation. *Homeless* merits more attention from Danish readers. If, as seems to be the case, the English version (entitled *Homeless, or a Poet's Inner Life*) is basically the work of Goldschmidt himself, it should be reprinted and made more readily available to Goldschmidt scholarship, especially since *Homeless* reveals more about Goldschmidt himself than do his other novels, and probably more than his memoirs. It cannot be passed over if an understanding of the psychology of the writer is to be achieved.

With the exception of *A Jew*, Goldschmidt's growing obsession with his idea of Nemesis as the principle of divine justice and order in the universe is apparent in all the longer works. Developing in *Homeless*, it becomes more definite in *The Heir* and is the central motive force in *The Raven*. After *The Raven* Goldschmidt wrote no more novels, and his energies were more and more taken up with his pseudo-scientific "researches" involving his Nemesis philosophy.

CHAPTER 3

Shorter Narrative Works

CLASSIFICATION of Goldschmidt's shorter literary works is difficult. Some are clearly short stories; some are novellas; some must be classified as fairy tales, although this term in English may be misleading. But others are mixtures of fact and fiction, or of realism and fantasy; some are difficult to classify merely because of their length. Goldschmidt's own identifications of some of his collections of narratives are at times confusing. He published several collections, which sometimes included works that had been printed previously. Some of the longer stories were separately published. In addition, Goldschmidt wrote two lengthy travel works which, because of interspersed stories and psychological portraits, as well as their literary language, are included among his belletristic works.

Goldschmidt's collections are entitled *Fortællinger* (*Stories* [1846]), *Blandede Skrifter* (*Mixed Writings* [1859–1860]), *Fortællinger og Skildringer* (*Stories and Descriptions* [1863–1865]), *Kjærlighedshistorier fra mange Lande* (*Love Stories from many Lands* [1867]), *Smaa Fortællinger* (*Little Stories* [1868–1869]), *Fortællinger og Virkelighedsbilleder, ældre og nye* (*Stories and Pictures of Reality, older and new* [1877]), *Fortællinger og Virkelighedsbilleder, Ny Samling* (*Stories and Pictures of Reality, New Collection* [1883]), and the posthumously published *Smaa Skildringer fra Fantasi og fra Virkelighed* (*Little Descriptions from Fantasy and from Reality* [1887]). Separately published were *Breve fra Choleratiden, indeholdende en lille Begivenhed* (*Letters from the Cholera Time, Containing a minor Incident* [1865]), reissued in 1867 with the title *En Roman i Breve* (*A Novel in Letters*); *Den Vægelsindede paa Graahede* (*The Fickle Girl on Graahede* [1867]); and *Avrohmche Nattergal* [1871]). The travel sketches were *Dagbog fra en Reise paa*

98

Vestkysten af Vendsyssel og Thy (Journal of a Trip on the West Coast of Vendsyssel and Thy [1865]) and *En Hedereise i Viborg-Egnen (A Trip on the Heath in the Viborg District* [1867]).

The first collection contained the cycle "Erindringer fra min Onkels Hus" ("Memories from my Uncle's House"), "For otte Skilling Hvedebrød" ("Eight Skillings' Worth of Wheat Bread"), "Aron og Esther" ("Aron and Esther"), and four frame-stories under the collective title "En Maifest" ("A May Celebration"). The frame-stories were "Drømmene" ("The Dreams"), "Watteaus Maleri" ("Watteau's Painting"), "Fortælling om en Flue" ("Story of a Fly"), and "Keiser Napoleon" ("Emperor Napoleon"). Goldschmidt later abandoned the frame, and the individual stories were subsequently reprinted without it.

"Memories from my Uncle's House" contains four stories or sketches written in the first person, all based on life in the household of Goldschmidt's own uncle, a merchant like Goldschmidt's father. All Jewish elements, however, have been omitted. The best of the stories, "Min Onkels Tømmerplads" (or "Tømmer-pladsen"—"My Uncle's Lumberyard") was first written for P. L. Møller's literary annual *Gæa* for the year 1846 (it appeared in December 1845), and at Møller's request, all specifically Jewish traits were avoided. "Tømmerpladsen" has become a classic of Danish literature. Like the other three sketches, it responded to a contemporary demand for local color in its description of a merchant's business establishment in a provincial market town. "Tømmerpladsen" is a sentimental story about suspicions of thievery from the lumberyard, which turn out to have been caused by the trysts of one of the apprentices with a neighbor's daughter, who crawls through a loose plank in the board fence surrounding the yard. There is the predictable happy ending, also a response to the popular taste. Language, style, and atmosphere, rather than any real originality in plot, have made this story and the others in the cycle live. *Memories from my Uncle's House* has been separately published, most recently in 1957. Goldschmidt's English reworking of parts of the cycle, under the title "My Uncle and his House: A Story of Danish Life," was published in 1863 in *Macmillan's Magazine*. "Lumber-yard" and "Eight Skillings Worth of Wheat Bread" were published in German translation in 1847.

"For otte Skilling Hvedebrød" ("Eight Skillings Worth of Wheat Bread") is a rather insipid story of a fortune's favorite, a poor boy who through lucky "coincidences" (an early stage on Goldschmidt's way toward Nemesis) makes his fortune in Brazil, and returns briefly to make his parents and sisters rich. A stronger foreshadowing of Nemesis is the figure of the boy's benefactor, who in his youth had seduced a girl in Brazil and had abandoned her and the daughter she had borne him. As a result of Nemesis, when he establishes another family in Denmark, his wife and son both die, and in his old age he realizes that he must rebalance the scales by returning to Brazil to care for the daughter. The boy follows him to Brazil when his studies are completed, only to learn that the old man has died. He remains there to become wealthy. In the first edition of the story, he marries the daughter of his benefactor, but in the later edition, Goldschmidt was evidently persuaded that this was one "chance" occurrence too many, even for Nemesis, and he omitted this detail.

"Aron and Esther" is the first of Goldschmidt's shorter Jewish stories. Aron is a young, attractive Jew who has violated Jewish ritual. He is to marry Esther, the daughter of a very pious Jew noted for his exemplary life. When Aron's transgression comes to light, he is in danger of losing Esther to a rival, but discovers that the rival, too, has violated ritual laws, and thus in the end wins her. Years later, Goldschmidt reworked "Aron and Esther" in English, and it was published in *Chambers's Journal* in 1863. The authentic and sympathetic rendering of the atmosphere surrounding Jewish life and culture was evidently something new to the English reading public, too; Goldschmidt wrote home from London that the story had been a great success, and that one of the founders of the periodical, Robert Chambers, had told him that he had broken a new path in English literature.[1] The concluding stories of the 1846 collection making up the frame-stories of "A May Celebration" are trifles, inferior to the other contents of the book.

In addition to the miscellaneous journalistic and political items contained in *Mixed Writings,* several earlier stories and sketches were reprinted here. Among these, the most representative are "Don Cleophas," which had appeared originally in *Nord og Syd* in 1856, and several Jewish legends—"Kongens Hjerne-skal" ("The King's Skull"), "Rabbi Meirs Hustru" ("Rabbi Meir's Wife"), "Rabbi Joschuah og Prindsessen" ("Rabbi Joschuah and the Princess"), "En græsk Philosoph og en Rabbi" ("A Greek Philosopher and a Rabbi"), "Rabbi Jochanni," "Mai-monides," "Rabbi Raschi," and "Den Gjerrige" ("The Miser")— some of which Goldschmidt was to make use of later. Most of them had appeared in *Nord og Syd* in 1852.

"Don Cleophas" is a fairy tale based on *Le diable boiteux* (1707) by Alain René Lesage (1668–1747). Goldschmidt's Don Cleophas is not a real devil but a spirit. When freed from a bottle in an abortive chemical experiment, he shows the hero details of private lives in Copenhagen, and explains that he does not have the power to forecast a person's fate absolutely, but only to predict what will happen if the person chooses one of two or more possible paths open to him at each juncture of his life. He promises to assist the hero in attaining worldly success if the hero will in turn use his influence to see that all spirits who have escaped from bottles will remain free. This seems to mean that the hero should do his utmost to see that high moral standards and aspirations are not compromised or suppressed for the sake of careers and success. In the second part of the story the hero forgets the spirit's advice, and devotes himself entirely to achieving success and wealth. His marriage to the woman the spirit had helped him to win becomes a mere form. Finally, on a trip to the Swiss mountains with Don Cleophas, who has returned to him for a time, he perishes in a crevasse in a glacier. Upon trying to enter heaven, he finds that his good deeds on earth are insufficient, and that he has been guilty of destroying the love which his wife had originally felt for him. She cannot help him into heaven, although she is to be admitted without question. Suddenly this all turns out to be only a dream, and he wakes up in his own home, with his wife speaking to him. He realizes that the spirit of good represented by Don Cleophas was within him, and that he has betrayed it; he now vows to be true to his youthful high moral values. Several years later Goldschmidt radically reworked "Don Cleophas" in Eng-lish, and the English version, entitled "The Elf's Ring," was printed serially in the British periodical *The Victoria Magazine* in 1864.

Goldschmidt was fond of Jewish legends and stories, and he sometimes tried to collect them on his travels. Most, however, were gleaned from his reading. He translated most of those printed in *Mixed Writings* into English and published them in *Chambers's Journal* in 1862, where he added several others, including "The Witnesses," which he had heard in the ghetto of Rome. The London *Jewish Chronicle and Hebrew Observer* reprinted it and identified the original source as Arabic. According to the *Jewish Chronicle,* most of Goldschmidt's "Hebrew Legends" had never before appeared in English. Goldschmidt later published the Danish version of "The Witnesses" in his sketch "Ghetto," which appeared in 1865. He subsequently used the Danish version of another of the English "Hebrew Legends"— "The Bird that sang to a Bridegroom"—in his collection *Love Stories from Many Lands* (1867).

The collection *Stories and Descriptions,* which contained material Goldschmidt had collected in Rome, appeared in three volumes, the third of which was taken up by the novel *The Heir.* The first volume, which came out in 1863, contained "Hvorledes man lever i Rom" ("How They Live in Rome"); the cycle "Hvorledes man fortæller i Rom ("How They Tell Stories in Rome"), consisting of the four stories "Photographierne og Mephistopheles" ("The Photographs and Mephistopheles"), "Den sidste Svovlstik" ("The Last Match"), "Ved St. Onofrio" ("At St. Onofrio"), and "Fortælling ved Frascati" ("Story near Frascati"); "En Jul paa Landet" ("A Christmas in the Country," which had been written originally in English); "En Dag i Flandern" ("A Day in Flanders"); "Molières 'Don Juan' "; and "Carnevalet" ("Carneval"). The second volume (1865) was made up of the following: "Beretning om ti Skandinavers Udflugt fra Via Felice til Ostia" ("Account of ten Scandinavians' Excursion from Via Felice to Ostia"), "Ghetto," "Peterskirkens Belysning" ("The Illumination of St. Peter's"), "Madonna," and a fifth story in the above mentioned cycle "Hvorledes man fortæller i Rom" entitled "En Soirée" ("A Soirée").

Some of the stories and sketches making up the first two volumes of *Stories and Descriptions* possess an interesting history and illustrate the complex relationship that at this time existed between Goldschmidt's English and Danish writings. In a letter from Rome in 1863, Goldschmidt wrote that the "Court's book dealer" ("Hoffets Boghandler," by whom he evidently meant Emily Faithfull, printer and publisher in ordinary to Queen Victoria and editor of *The Victoria Magazine*) had agreed to publish his short stories, most of which were ready, and that he would complete the collection when he returned to London.[2] Emily Faithfull did in fact publish the English versions of several of the stories and sketches of *Stories and Descriptions* in her *Victoria Magazine,* and although they did not appear until 1868, it would seem that Goldschmidt actually wrote them first in English. A note in *The Victoria Magazine,* appended to the stories, states that the stories were "original tales now published for the first time."[3] A long delay in publication seems not to have been uncommon with *The Victoria Magazine*—Goldschmidt wrote of being occupied with reworking "Don Cleophas" in English in September 1861,[4] but the English version finally appeared in that journal in 1864.

The titles of the English versions of the stories from *Stories and Descriptions* which appeared in *The Victoria Magazine* were "The Last Lucifer Match," "The Photographs and Mephistopheles," and "At St. Onofrio—Tasso's Life." Two other selections were added; one was a reworking of older material and the other, "Rabbi Akiba," never appeared in Danish; Goldschmidt must have written it in English and never translated it into Danish.

The cycle "How They Tell Stories in Rome" is another series of frame-stories, told in the "Society of Virtue" ("Dydsforeningen"); the collective title of the English versions is "The Society of Virtue at Rome." Emily Faithfull issued a separate offprint of the collection under that title in 1868. The two most outstanding stories, which occur in both English and Danish versions, are "The Last Lucifer Match" and "The Photographs and Mephistopheles."

"The Last Lucifer Match" combines two of Goldschmidt's recurrent themes, Nemesis and honorable versus dishonorable love. The story, told by a Dane-become-Scotsman at a meeting of the "Society," purports to concern a friend who has arranged a rendezvous with a pure and naive Scots girl with the purpose of seducing her, and then finds himself lost on the Scottish moors in a snowstorm with a group of his friends. They can save themselves from freezing to death only if they can light a fire in a cave where they find shelter. They discover, however, that all their matches are wet. Then one of the party finds one last match. Before trying to light it, he begins to say the Lord's Prayer. As the prayer progresses, the narrator suddenly feels that he is on trial, that it is his fault that the whole party is in danger, and that only he can save them. He does not know how, until as the prayer is drawing to an end, he suddenly understands that his intended seduction of the innocent girl is being punished in advance. He resolves to marry the girl instead of seducing her, and immediately feels secure. The prayer ends, the match lights, and they are saved. Of course, the "friend" is the Scots-Dane himself, and Goldschmidt makes this clear in a masterful little touch where he has the narrator suddenly shift from third person to first person, without drawing attention to the shift.

The genesis of "The Photographs and Mephistopheles" is related in a letter which Goldschmidt wrote to Hester Rothschild from Rome.[5] The night before, he had been having tea with a Norwegian family, and one of the daughters had shown him the family collection of photographs, not gathered into an album, but consisting of loose pictures spread out on a table. The idea for a story had suddenly occurred to Goldschmidt, and he explained in detail in the letter the plot of the proposed tale. Curiously, he writes that he thinks the story can be written only in Danish, "for the English public take no interest in such things." Obviously, he was wrong on both counts. Once again, the story is told at a meeting of the "Society of Virtue." The narrator has seen some unrelated photographs of tourists in a shop window, and imagines that they are living people, gathered at random. Mephistopheles joins them, and promises each of them a wish, which will cost the price which he will write on a slip of paper for each. One of the men cannot make up his mind what to wish for, but the others all have wishes; the price for each proves to be "life." The meaning is that any desire worth pursuing will require devoting one's entire life to it; if one has no goal at all to pursue, this too will cost a life, in that one's life will then be wasted.

"A Christmas in the Country" was originally written in English in 1862, while Goldschmidt was living in London, and he mentions the story several times in his letters of that and the following year. It was a source of great disappointment to him that he was not able to get it published in England. On his way from London to Rome in 1863, he stopped off in Paris, and went to see Charles Dickens, who was in Paris at the time, to ask for his help in getting the story published, probably in Dickens' journal *All the Year Round*. Dickens, however, did not respond to Goldschmidt's letter or the visiting card which he had left at Dickens' address, and Goldschmidt left Paris without seeing Dickens. He then decided to translate the story into Danish and included it in the material from Rome.

The story, told in the first person, is a simple one. The narrator is invited by an old schoolmate to spend the Christmas holidays at the latter's newly inherited estate. An old teacher of theirs is also invited. The school comrade's sweetheart is in danger of being forced to marry her cousin, one of the neighboring landowner's six oversized sons. The narrator, with the aid of an actress who had been a pupil of the old school teacher (a noncoincidence), hoodwinks the would-be bridegroom, and the real sweethearts are brought together. The subplot, an injustice inflicted on a tenant farmer by the landowner's son, was based on an actual incident which Goldschmidt had described earlier in *Nord og Syd*.

Of the other items in the first two volumes of *Stories and Descriptions*, "Ghetto" is of interest since it too was apparently written first in English; in a letter to Hester Rothschild in May 1864, Goldschmidt wrote, "The Ghetto is progressing in English."[6] It did not appear in Danish until 1865. "The Illumination of St. Peter's" is of importance since it seems to give an indication of Goldschmidt's feelings for Mrs. Stilling. "A Soirée," a continuation of the cycle "How They Tell Stories in Rome," contains three frame-stories, but the frame is of more interest than the stories; the stories are told in the salon of Marie Espérance von Schwartz (née Brandt), the English-born writer of travel books and friend of Garibaldi (see p. 50 above). In 1863 she was still in Rome and presided over an intellectual salon which was frequented particularly by foreigners. Details of Goldschmidt's acquaintance with her are not known, but he called her "my elderly friend" in writing to Hester Rothschild.

The idea for the collection *Love Stories from many Lands* came to Goldschmidt during the winter of 1866. Originally it was to have been a collection of translations, but when Goldschmidt began searching for examples, he could not find what he wanted, so he decided to compose them himself. He asked the Norwegian writer Bjørnstjerne Bjørnson for a Norwegian love story, but Bjørnson never contributed any, although several of Goldschmidt's love stories were printed in Bjørnson's *Norske Folkeblad* in 1867. In the introduction to the collection, Goldschmidt wrote that although some of the stories had been written previously, the poetic stimulus for the collection came while he was visiting the 1867 world's exposition in Paris. He and a group of his friends stopped to drink coffee at an Arab stand, and the Arab waiter was asked to tell a story. He agreed to do so, if Goldschmidt would tell one first. Both told a little tale, and Goldschmidt decided to collect those he had already written, add to them, and publish them together.

The collection included "Den polske Kongesøn" ("The Polish Prince"), "Paolo og Giovanna" ("Paolo and Giovanna"), "Patrick O'Brien og Cathleen," "Henry Cecil og Sarah," "Billedhuggeren" ("The Sculptor"), "Senki," "Lureley," "Fuglen der sang" ("The Bird that Sang"), "Assar og Mirjam," "Guds Engel fra Rørvig" ("God's Angel from Rørvig"), "Henrik og Rosalie," "Genremaleren" ("The Genre Painter"), "Hertugen af Villa-Medina" ("The Duke of Villa-Medina"), and "Sidi-el-Barduk og Zuleima." "Fuglen der sang" had appeared originally in English, under the title "The Bird that sang to a Bridegroom," in 1862 in *Chambers's Journal*. Most of the stories are very short; all express aspects of love; some end happily, some unhappily. Almost all are charming miniatures.

Two of the finest of the love stories are "Paolo and Giovanna" and "God's Angel from Rørvig." The first is only four pages long. Paolo, a young man of Padua, is hopelessly in love but never has the opportunity of declaring himself to Giovanna, his beloved, and she marries another. Consumed by his love for her,

Paolo asks her husband for permission to see her, without speaking to her. The husband, his vanity flattered, agrees. When Paolo looks at Giovanna, his eyes betray him, and she at once realizes that he loves her, and she returns his love. But she is conscious of the hopelessness of their passion. When she attends mass with her husband, she eludes him long enough to consecrate herself to the Church. Ten years pass, and the nun feels the approach of death. She goes to confession, and to the monk in the confessional she tells of her love for Paolo, and asks for the miracle of seeing him once more before she dies. The monk tells her to look at him through the grating of the confessional. The other nuns hear a cry from the confessional, and later, alarmed by the long silence, they discover the monk and the nun, still sitting in the confessional, dead. Although the conclusion is obvious, Goldschmidt, showing his usual delicate artistic taste, leaves it up to the reader to draw it.

"God's Angel from Rørvig" is the nickname of the eighteen-year-old daughter of a customs official of that village on the northern coast of Zealand; she is so called by the villagers because as a child she had been sickly and had been cured as if by the collective affection of all the villagers. When a Danish privateer captain brings in a prize, captured from the British, within sight of the village, he is invited to stay with the customs official. He and the girl fall in love, but when he asks her to leave with him, she refuses. In her garden the girl has planted an offshoot of a neighbor's mulberry tree. She insists on transplanting it, and a few days later she finds that it has died, unable to live after being torn from its native spot of soil. To the girl this is an obvious omen; nevertheless, when the captain sails, she leaves with him, unable to withstand the imperative of love. The omen proves to be true, and ten days later the girl dies. In an epilogue it is reported that the captain returns to Rørvig to stay, and builds a house near the spot where the girl had waited to elope with him. The villagers soon nickname him "God's devil from the sea," without, however, implying any antipathy. Nemesis is present in the story, but not as punishment for a "sin"; the girl knows what fate is in store for her, but chooses to pay the price demanded for her great love for the captain. This price is collected, and the books are balanced.

Love Stories from many Lands was soon translated into German (1879) and into Russian (1889). "Assar and Mirjam," "Henrik and Rosalie," and "Paolo and Giovanna" have appeared in English translation. The collection was reprinted in Danish most recently in 1959; "The Polish Prince" was reprinted separately in 1962.

Smaa Fortællinger (*Little Stories*) contained two of Goldschmidt's masterpieces which exemplify two very different types of prose composition—"Maser" (one-tenth of an acquired sum which, according to Jewish law, must be paid to the needy), the most charming of Goldschmidt's Jewish short stories; and "Bjergtagen I" ("Bewitched I") best described in English as a fairy tale. The collection, first published in fascicles, also contained "Den flyvende Post" ("Flying Mail"), "Hævnen" ("Revenge"), "Bjergtagen II," "I en Postvogn" ("In a Stage-coach"), and "Ekko'et" ("The Echo").

"Maser" brought the unforgettable Simon Levi, the little Jewish agent from *The Raven*, back to the Danish reading public. He was simply too interesting a character for Goldschmidt to leave alone. The reader is introduced to Levi's intimate circle—to his spinster sister Gidel, who is also his housekeeper, and to his brash brother Mortche (who has Christianized his name to Martin, to Simon's disgust). Levi suddenly learns of the death of the friend of his youth in South America (introduced in *The Raven*), and of the latter's having willed him a large sum of money. Mortche is perpetually on the verge of bankruptcy, although he puts on a show of affluence, and Gidel makes the point that Simon will have to give a tenth of his inheritance to the needy, and it might as well be to their brother, who well qualifies. Simon, however, resists stubbornly, since he disapproves of his brother's lighthearted attitude toward money, and even more of his relaxed treatment of Jewish tradition. Meanwhile, Simon finds that his new riches cannot really change his own station, and he cannot qualify as a member of the upper class. He gives away smaller sums as partial payment of "maser," in the hope that this will suffice to God. Gidel falls dangerously ill and must undergo an operation. Mortche, in the meantime, is faced with immediate ruin, if he cannot borrow a sum exactly equalling one-tenth of Simon's inheritance (Nemesis). Simon senses the hand of God in this, and when he sees the Christian doctor, the best surgeon available, making the sign of the cross over his surgical instruments while preparing for the operation, he capitulates and promises the money to Mortche. Gidel is saved, Mortche avoids ruin, and Mortche's son can now marry the girl of his choice, even though she has no fortune. Once Simon has acknowledged his "guilt" and has accepted the power of Nemesis, his own inner balance and harmony, and that of his world, is restored.

"Maser" is Goldschmidt at his best. The triumph of characterization in *The Raven* is repeated and surpassed. Despite the overly sentimental ending, the story remains a masterpiece, and in spite of the hand of Nemesis, the realism of the presentation of the Jewish milieu and the believable and human depiction of Simon Levi's psychology are irresistible. The story is a classic and has been reprinted numerous times in collections, most recently in 1961. It has been translated into German several times, both separately and in an anthology, and has also been translated into Russian and Yiddish.

In "Bewitched I" the lady of a manor is subjected to the conflict between the dictates of her erotic attraction for a poetic, supernatural being and the demands of her duty to her prosaic but devoted husband. She follows her mysterious lover to his realm, but is forced to return to her husband when he appeals to "law" (Nemesis) which must be obeyed, even at the cost of the destruction of the supernatural world and the manor house, the life of the lady, and the loss of the happiness of the man. The material was not original with Goldschmidt—the basic idea for the narrative came from Jørgen Moe, the Norwegian collector of folktales, who had told Goldschmidt a similar story. Goldschmidt was also influenced by a story of the Danish provincial writer Steen Steensen Blicher (1782–1848), "Rødstenen paa Fur" ("The Red Rock on Fur"; Fur is an island in the Limfjord). It is once again the language and the style that make Goldschmidt's story original and memorable; his descriptions of sounds—for example, of the ice "bells" on the banks of the pond in the winter, and of the many murmurings in the garden and the trees in the summer—are poetry. It is this that makes "Bewitched I" such enjoyable reading, rather than Goldschmidt's message of the inescapability of Nemesis (in this case equated with duty) and the insoluble conflict between fantasy and reality. The story has been translated into English, French, and Dutch, and was reprinted in Denmark as recently as 1971.

Of the other stories in *Little Stories,* "Bjergtagen II" ("Bewitched II") also concerns the conflict between fantasy and reality. The hero ends by eternally riding back and forth between the girl of his fantasy and the girl of reality, unable to make up his mind between them. "Flying Mail" is a trifle, expressing once again Goldschmidt's thesis that there is no such thing as pure chance. The hero writes a love letter and entrusts it to the wind, but it finds its way to the girl best suited for him. The story has been translated into English and reprinted several times, most recently in 1970. "Revenge" sets forth Goldschmidt's belief that personal revenge for a wrong only leads to further wrongs, and that Nemesis takes care of righting wrongs. "In a Stagecoach" presents a series of frame-stories and legends, told by three Jewish merchants on their way to an auction. "The Echo" is one of Goldschmidt's Jutland stories. It combines local color and local folktale elements with the action of Nemesis. The hero challenges fate and is punished by being separated from his sweetheart and by being falsely accused of wrongdoing. He is redeemed when he recognizes his mistake, whereupon he is reunited with his true love, and Nemesis overtakes the real wrongdoer.

Fortællinger og Virkelighedsbilleder, ældre og nye (*Stories and Pictures of Reality, older and new*) contained for the most part items which had already appeared in print. The story "Gift" ("Poison") is an exception. It was published the same year as *Life's Recollections and Results,* the last part of which is devoted to Goldschmidt's work on Nemesis, and the story is an expression of the action of Nemesis in a subtle, refined form. "Poison" is a double first-person narrative—the first narrator (Goldschmidt) accidentally meets a man he had previously known slightly, and is invited to stay at the latter's home. He meets the man's wife, and is struck by the atmosphere of peace and harmony present in the household. The husband comments that he and his wife have built their home on truth and candor, and that they have attained something approaching perfection in absolute mutual understanding and harmony. This is his first mistake in challenging fate, and he makes another in unthinkingly comparing his wife to a character in literature who ultimately drowns herself, for in Goldschmidt's philosophy of Nemesis, one is responsible for the words one unthinkingly utters, and even for the heedless words one listens to.

The two men meet some time later, and the husband becomes the narrator in the first person, telling the story of his life. As a young man, he was engaged as a tutor for the girl who was later to become his wife, at that time a girl of thirteen. At a neighboring wealthy estate, the style of life maintained by the husband (the wife was for the most part restricted by poor health to her rooms) and his friends was frivolous and loose. The young girl's mother, as well as her two older sisters, had already been "poisoned" by being constantly invited to the wealthy estate, and the girl's father wanted to prevent his youngest daughter from being "poisoned" along with them. He had decided to hire a tutor who would have absolute authority over the girl. The young tutor succeeded, in the course of several years, in overcoming the girl's initial hatred for him (as a result of his thwarting her plans to escape to the uncontrolled life of the wealthy manor), and in apparently "curing" her of the yearning for the life of the manor. Eventually they had fallen in love and had married. For years they led a happy and apparently well-adjusted life together. Suddenly, however, when she was over thirty years old, she was again seized with the uncontrollable desire for the frivolous life, and in her husband's absence she became infatuated with one of his business friends, and eventually asked the friend to run away with her to America. When the man refused, she returned home, and told her children not to tell their father that she had been away. She realized suddenly that she had betrayed the principle of truth on which her family had been established. Unable to continue living with untruth, she drowned herself. The husband now recognizes his own guilt in challenging fate, and accepts Nemesis' action in humbling him.

Unlike Goldschmidt's previous collection, *Fortællinger og Virkelighedsbilleder, Ny Samling* (*Stories and Pictures of Reality, New Collection*), contained largely new material, as he points out in a foreword. In it were "Fortælling om to Børn eller Hvordan Mdm. Skau fik sin Vilje" ("Story of two Children, or how Mme. Skau got her Way"), "Levi og Ibald" ("Levi and Ibald"), "Mendel Hertz," "De Skilte: Billede fra en Reise" ("The Estranged Couple: Travel Picture"), "I en Bjergegn" ("In a Mountain Region"), "En sær Reise" ("A Strange Trip"), and "En Dampskibstur" ("A Steamer Trip"). Only the first three add anything significant to the body of Goldschmidt's work. "Story of two Children" is a long sentimental story of a working-class mother who has lofty plans for her son, and when he shows signs of falling in love with a girl whom the mother considers beneath him, she schemes repeatedly to keep the two young people apart. Thanks, however, to the "laws" of Goldschmidt's Nemesis, the boy and the girl are brought together in spite of the mother, and by this time the girl is a successful artist and is thus acceptable even to the mother. "Levi and Ibald" brings back the Jewish agent and the would-be poet from *The Raven* again. Levi is caught up in the religious unrest of the time, with its anti-Semitism, and sees Jewish tradition eroded from within, with his nephew's ignoring many of the Jewish tenets. Levi takes Ibald into his home as insurance against what he sees as signs of a new wave of persecution, but this act brings on a chain of circumstances which accidentally lead to Levi's tragicomic death. Goldschmidt's own attitude toward the spirit of the times here seems somewhat ambiguous. The story has not been translated into English; a Russian translation appeared in 1913.

"Mendel Hertz," the last of Goldschmidt's Jewish stories, is slighter than the others. Mendel is a poor, slightly misshapen shoemaker whose cheerless existence is momentarily brightened when he mistakenly believes that the young stepdaughter of his aunt is in love with him. He goes to propose to her, just in time to hear of her engagement to her real sweetheart. The disappointment eventually causes his death, Unlike the other Jewish stories, "Mendel Hertz" does not express any conflict between the Jewish and the Christian worlds. It has been repeatedly reprinted in Danish, most recently in 1961, and has been translated into English (1937).

Goldschmidt's last collection of short stories, *Smaa Skildringer fra Fantasi og fra Virkelighed* (*Little Descriptions from Fantasy and from Reality*) was to have been the writer's offering to his public, commemorating the fiftieth anniversary of his first appearance as a writer (3 October 1837, with the *Nestved Ugeblad*), but Goldschmidt died in August. His son Adolf, by this time a medical doctor, arranged for publication in his father's memory. The collection consists of various short compositions which were among Goldschmidt's papers, most of them written during the last few years of his life. According to Goldschmidt's foreword, "Af Erik Vidførles Saga" ("From Erik the Far-Traveler's Saga"), however, was written around 1860. The full contents were "En lille Dreng" ("A Little Boy"), "En lille Pige" ("A Little Girl"), "Lirekassen" ("The Barrel Organ"), "Næsten et Geni" ("Almost a Genius"), "Tilfældigt Møde" ("Chance Encounter"), "Et Gjensyn" ("A Meeting"), "'Masaniello,'" "Uløst" ("Unsolved"), "Af Erik Vidførles Saga," "Hvad der var i Hilda Hydes Bylt" ("What there was in Hilda Hyde's Bundle"), "Fra Arcachon" ("From Arcachon"), "Pech" ("Bad Luck"), and "Et Væddeløb" ("A Horserace"). None added any new facets to Goldschmidt's fame, but "Uløst" ("Unsolved") might be considered Goldschmidt's contribution to the Scandinavian literary feud over sexual morals and the double standard in marriage which was taking place at this time. According to the foreword, "Unsolved" was actually written in 1882, when the controversy was in its early stages. In "Unsolved" the narrator reads to a small group of friends a fragment of a play he is writing. The scene depicts a marriage proposal, in which the man admits to an affair in his past. The woman, reciprocating his frankness, also confesses to a love affair in her past. The narrator then asks his listeners how they would finish the scene—whether the man would pursue his marriage proposal or withdraw it. They are unable to agree, and the ultimate "solution" is the suggestion that two endings be written for the play, to be staged on alternate nights. The ingenious "solution" could be interpreted as an outgrowth of Goldschmidt's broadmindedness, but it could likewise be construed as proceeding from a consciousness of his own youthful affair and *pro forma* marriage with Johanne Sonne.

Of the separately published shorter works, *Breve fra Cholera-*

tiden (*Letters from the Cholera Time*), although entitled *En Roman i Breve* (*A Novel in Letters*) in its second edition, does not conform to modern definitions of a novel. Once again Goldschmidt was demonstrating the action of Nemesis in the man-woman relationship, as well as showing that there are no chance occurrences in life.

The letters, by Ernst Rosen, a former poet and now a civil servant, Frants Holm, a painter, and the latter's friend Mathiesen, are supposedly written during the actual cholera epidemic of 1853, but the epidemic only provides a backdrop for the events described. The story is primarily one of Rosen's search for the perfect woman of his fantasy, his temporary engagement to a false symbol of this perfection, and eventually his finding its true embodiment. Secondary lines of the story are provided by Rosen's earlier abandonment of poetry for a more secure career as a civil servant, and then his abandonment of that career in turn for a more satisfying life as, apparently, an enlightened director of a factory; and by Holm's engagement to the girl of his choice. An afterword brings forward the fiction that Goldschmidt is only the publisher, not the author, of the letters, as he meets the protagonists several years later and is told their story and given the permission to publish their letters. The same problems are presented as in *Homeless*—the principal character's search for inner harmony and his quest for the embodiment of his idea of the perfect woman. Unlike Otto in *Homeless*, however, he finds both in time to live and enjoy them.

Den Vægelsindede paa Graahede (*The Fickle Girl on Graahede*) is, like "The Echo," a result of Goldschmidt's visits to Jutland. The story was based on local family traditions, and the model for Karen, the heroine, was a real person. Karen is a complex personality, and the story is a psychological study of a woman whose character is controlled by erotic forces she does not understand. When she was a child of confirmation age, her family's farmstead was visited by a professor with a group to whom he lectured on the historical events that had taken place on and around the farmstead. He asked Karen to be their guide, and in speaking to her, had stroked her head. This unaccustomed touch and the half-understood words of the professor left her with vague, unclear impulses that affect her psycho-

logical development long after the incident itself is forgotten.
When she grows up, she is unable to decide which of her
suitors she will accept as a husband. At first she is on the point
of accepting her first suitor, Jens, but suddenly abandons him
for another, an action she goes on repeating until her father
calls a halt to her flightiness. Her suitor of the moment, however, releases her from her word, and Jens renews his suit. In
the meantime, humiliated each time she has changed suitors,
he has sworn several oaths to have his revenge on her. The
last oath, by which Jens feels absolutely bound, is to hitch
her to his plow. After they are finally married, he harnesses
her to the plow, but although she recognizes that she has
wronged Jens, she would prefer to be beaten to death rather
than to submit to this degradation. Torn between his genuine
love for her and the oath which he feels is inescapable, he solves
the dilemma by harnessing himself beside her, and she now
readily agrees to pull the plow with him. Goldschmidt has here
combined his firsthand knowledge of Blicher's province with
local traditions and folklore (the idea of hitching a recalcitrant
or unfaithful wife to a farm implement seems to have occurred
to widely differing cultures) and with his customary Nemesis
motif (Karen's stubborn will must encounter an equally adamant
spirit, then both must be humbled; Jens is "punished" because
of the arrogance of his oath).

Avrohmche Nattergal, separately published in 1871, was to
have been Goldschmidt's last Jewish story, and contained his
own "comic or grotesque" picture of "Jewish blood's infatuation
with the heathen-Christian world."[7] The character of "Little
Abraham Nightingale" was, according to Goldschmidt, based
on a childhood memory of a visit to the theater, where he had
met a Jewish ticket scalper called Avrohmche Schnorr.[8] Goldschmidt's Avrohmche is the son of a moderately successful
merchant who wants his son to take over the business after
him. Avrohmche, however, is drawn to music and singing, but
his father ridicules him so much that he gives up all thought
of a stage career. Irresistibly attracted to the theater, he rents
a box there and sells tickets to it, neglecting his father's business.
This results in his father's expelling him with the prediction
that the theater will be the cause of Avrohmche's hanging him-

self. Avrohmche's only friends are the family Sass (their name
had originally been "Suss," which means "horse" in Hebrew).
As the Sass family's prosperity increases, they hire a Christian
maid. Avrohmche had at one time proposed to the only Sass
daughter, Gitte, but had been rejected. This has not disturbed
the good relations between Avrohmche and the Sass family,
however. Avrohmche, by this time middle-aged, falls in love
with the Christian maid. He gives her a ticket to his box at
the theater. In his fantasy, they are already married, and when
a young man makes advances to the girl, Avrohmche involun-
tarily calls out that she is his wife. She reacts with shame and
embarrassment, and Avrohmche, crushed, goes home and tries
to hang himself. He is cut down and taken to a hospital, however.
Gitte's mother, startled into action by the vague rumors that
Avrohmche is married (in the crowd at the theater, no one
had associated Avrohmche with the maid), or is about to be,
suddenly remembers that she has an aging unmarried daughter,
and that Avrohmche has inherited some money from his father.
She decides that Gitte and Avrohmche should be married. Gitte
confesses to Avrohmche that she once, twenty years earlier (at
the time Avrohmche had asked for her hand), had been in
love with a Christian officer, whereupon Avrohmche also confesses his infatuation. There is mutual forgiveness and a presumed happy ending.

Besides reflecting Goldschmidt's own ambivalent attitude
toward the Christian world, *Avrohmche Nattergal* shows Nemesis
in a refined form. Avrohmche and Gitte both "belong" in the
Jewish world, and they "belong" to each other. But Gitte's
errant infatuation with the Christian officer early prevented
their union, and only after twenty years and Avrohmche's transgression and sufferings do they acquire the resignation that
enables them to accept each other. For his part, Avrohmche has
failed his father, just as he failed his own dream of becoming
an artist, and since he has failed at everything in life, it is only
just (Nemesis) that he fail in his attempt at suicide. His fate
and that of Gitte are again in balance.

Avrohmche Nattergal has been one of Goldschmidt's most
popular stories in Denmark, and has been reprinted several
times, both separately and in anthologies, as recently as 1961.

It has likewise appeared in German translation both separately
(1875) and anthologized, and has been translated into both
Russian (1913) and English (1928). The English translation
has been reprinted in anthologies several times, most recently
in 1965.

In Goldschmidt's memoirs is included a little story entitled
"Slaget ved Marengo" ("The Battle at Marengo") which Goldschmidt reports that he found among some of his old papers.[9]
He was unable to remember exactly when it had been written; it
had not been used previously. His expressed modest opinion
of the story is not justified—it is a charming little political satire.
"The Battle at Marengo" is the account of an accident which
befalls the mayor of a provincial market town. The mayor, in
crossing a ditch on a board, slips and breaks his leg. There are
two contributing causes—he had lost a suspender button and
is hampered in taking long steps, and the shoemaker's son had
moved the board slightly. The whole town is divided into two
parties, the button party and the board party. At that time,
the French Revolution and its aftermath absorb the world's
attention, and the town's two parties follow the events through
the newspaper that reaches the town once a week. When
Napoleon wins the battle of Marengo, a dispatch rider brings
the news, and although both parties want to shout for joy, each
refuses to exhibit emotion in front of the other, and the universal
cheer dies before it is born. From that time on, the town slowly
dies. But the dispatch rider becomes postmaster.

In writing his travel books, *Dagbog fra en Reise paa Vestkysten af Vendsyssel og Thy* (*Journal of a Trip on the West
Coast of Vendsyssel and Thy* [1865]) and *En Hedereise i Viborg-
Egnen* (*A Trip on the Heath in the Viborg District* [1867]),
Goldschmidt was following a long international literary tradition.
Goldschmidt combined the abilities of a journalist and an imaginative writer; his travel sketches are absorbing and informa-
tive; in addition they are written in an effortless and flowing
style. Goldschmidt was always a close and accurate observer
of human types and psychologies, and his descriptions of people
are more interesting than his descriptions of places and historical
events. The latter can become somewhat tedious to the modern
non-Danish reader. Before his productive stays in London and

Rome in the early 1860s, Goldschmidt had been ignorant of the areas of central and western Jutland, and he was probably influenced in his desire to see them by Mrs. Stilling in Rome (her husband of the time owned an estate in that part of Denmark). By the nature of the travel descriptions, the works have not attracted the attention of translators, although a new Danish edition of *A Trip on the Heath* appeared in 1954.

The dominant themes in Goldschmidt's shorter works are the same that recur continually in his novels; they also represent Goldschmidt's own problems, which occupied him in his personal life as much as they did in his writing: the incompatibility of the Jewish and Christian worlds; the conflict between the sexes, involving Goldschmidt's never-attained fantasy of female perfection; the (predominantly male) struggle for self-fulfillment; and, increasingly with the years, the pervasive presence of Nemesis intertwining with the other themes, superimposing itself upon all other problems, complicating them and at the same time solving them or rendering them irrelevant.

CHAPTER 4

Dramatic Works

G OLDSCHMIDT'S dramatic works have been unjustly ne-
glected. They have not been reprinted in this century, and
since Julius Salomon excluded them from his edition of Goldschmidt's selected works (published 1908–1910) and still the
"standard" edition, they have been overlooked or dismissed as
not significant. They are in fact far from insignificant, and must
be taken into account in any study of Goldschmidt and his work.
They all appeared during the 1860s, at the height of Goldschmidt's productivity.

Goldschmidt had always been deeply interested in the theater—even during his *Corsaren* period he had written concerning
the contemporary theater in Copenhagen, and his later reviews
in *Nord og Syd* demonstrate a developed theatrical sense, as
well as an awareness that the Danish theater was in a state
of relative stagnation. During his trips to London he was a
frequent visitor to the theater, and he translated several contemporary English plays into Danish; these translations were
staged in Copenhagen.

The immediate stimulus for Goldschmidt's turning to writing
for the stage may have come from the noted actor Christen
Niemann Rosenkilde (see p. 54 above). Goldschmidt's first published dramatic work, *Rabbi Eliezer,* was completed in London
in 1861. In its original form, it was not intended for the stage,
but was a so-called closet drama (that is, to be read), as the
author makes clear in a foreword. Two of Goldschmidt's ob-
sessive themes once more appear in this work—the power of
Nemesis, and the irreconcilable conflict between Christian society
and Jewish culture. Incidentally, *Rabbi Eliezer* contains examples of Goldschmidt's rare use of verse.

Rabbi Eliezer, whose wife had been killed by the Christians,

119

and whose son had been abducted by them, is wandering in search of his son. The scene is the town of Andernach in the fourteenth century. Eliezer arrives as the knights and soldiers are returning from wars with the Turks, and he is greeted by the Jewish community (Jews are allowed to live and carry on trade here, at the cost of a large annual tribute). The returning army is led by Bertrand, a Christian knight who has covered himself with glory in the wars and is betrothed to Isabella, the daughter of a nobleman. A disturbance breaks out in the Jewish quarter, caused by a Christian drunken good-for-nothing, and Isabella's father is injured by a rock. Bertrand is entrusted with the punishment of the Jews, who are blamed for starting an uprising, and he is to pass judgment on the surviving Jewish leaders. The first to be brought before him is Eliezer, who recognizes Bertrand as his son, abducted years before. He assumes that Bertrand will now abandon Christianity and return to Judaism, and will escape with him. Bertrand, however, is bound by too many ties to Christendom, particularly by his love for Isabella, and renounces his father. In a memorable scene Eliezer pronounces a curse on his son—in Judaism a powerful act, and one which Goldschmidt had used before, one which he had himself witnessed as a boy when an uncle had cursed Goldschmidt's father. Bertrand, horrified, orders his father taken safely out of the castle. He then goes to his wedding with Isabella, unable to tell her what has just happened.

As time passes, Bertrand feels the effects of the curse. His former friends turn against him, and though he defeats them at first, he foresees the ultimate disaster awaiting him. Now regretting his curse, Eliezer tries to find a way to nullify it, but soon realizes that it is irrevocable. He too is caught up in it, since he has also transgressed against God (Nemesis) by setting in motion the destruction of his own son. To restore order to their world, Nemesis must punish both father and son. In the scene of the meeting between Eliezer and Ilse, a Christian woman whose son has been killed in the wars, Goldschmidt gives a superbly understated contrast between Judaism, with its unforgiving, punitive philosophy and Christianity, with its doctrine of forgiveness. Ilse would be willing to see her son renounce her and her faith, if only he could be restored to life, while Eliezer must regard his son as dead although he is alive and well. Among Goldschmidt's papers from this period preserved in the Royal Library, Copenhagen, is an English translation of this scene, written in Goldschmidt's own hand; Goldschmidt evidently intended at the time to publish the work in English also.

Ilse and Eliezer are surprised by a group of surviving Jews, who have taken to the woods and are seeking both revenge and restoration of their rights. One recognizes Ilse who, half-mad, had incited the Christian rabble to plunder and slaughter the Jewish community, since she resented the fact that their children were still alive. A Jew who had lost his sister in the attack kills Ilse, and is himself taken away in bonds by the other Jews.

The Jews, who blame Bertrand for the slaughter of their community, betray to Bertrand's enemies an underground entrance to his stronghold. When the attacking Christian knight demands a hostage of the Jews, Eliezer offers himself. When the enemy knight attacks, Eliezer willingly takes the first blow, thus saving his son at the price of his own life. Bertrand, after killing his father's slayer, leaves his wife and castle to wander in search of his people and his past. Nemesis has restored order in the world, and the curse has run its course by destroying both its object and its originator.

Goldschmidt's next dramatic work was *Svedenborgs Ungdom* (*Swedenborg's Youth* [1863]).[1] The idea for the work came, according to Goldschmidt's afterword, from a brief note in the English biography of Swedenborg by J. J. G. Wilkinson. This work described very briefly the only love Swedenborg is supposed to have had, and Goldschmidt was prompted to fill in details of Swedenborg's emotions and reactions to the abrupt ending of his romance.

Svedenborg, twenty-five years old at the time and in love with a fifteen-year-old girl, easily persuades the girl's father to sign a document promising to him the girl, whom he tutors. The girl does not want to marry him, and the document is stolen, whereupon Svedenborg willingly relinquishes his claim upon her. He vows, however, that her presence will accompany him throughout his life. Nemesis, whose presence is implied in Svedenborg's loss of the document (since it would have been unjust to force the girl into a marriage with him), is glaringly present in the love story of the cavalry officer Sparre, and Svedenborg offers one of Goldschmidt's definitions of Nemesis: "the great justice in heaven and on earth" ("den store Retfærd .i Himlen og paa Jorden"). As Hans Kyrre has pointed out, the characters in the drama have no fixed, concrete exterior; the whole work is shadowy and the dialogue is really a series of monologues.[2]

The first of Goldschmidt's dramatic works actually to reach the stage was *En Skavank* (*A Flaw* [1867]). Before its premiere on 6 September 1867, it had a long and varied history (see pp. 54–55). *A Flaw*, a three-act play with a prelude, is devoted to the action of Nemesis. Early in his career, Severin, a successful attorney, has been the cause of a man's ruin in a transaction which was technically legal but ethically immoral. This has resulted in his "flaw," an uneasy conscience. He has tried to make good his action by supporting the ruined man's son until he has expended the exact sum which caused the father's ruin. Severin then attempts to halt his support of the young man, but Goldschmidt's Nemesis is never content with bookkeeping of this sort, but requires full and open acknowledgment of a transgression before the moral scales are again in balance. Once this confession has taken place, a happy ending can occur.

A Flaw was a success and was staged fourteen times in 1867–1868. As the theatrical historian Edgar Collin (1836–1906) described the production,[3] its success was probably due more to the superb performances of some of the cast than to the action of the play, since this was slow-moving and the situations were not dramatic. It was really a story rather than a play, but the witty, pointed lines, typical of Goldschmidt's prose writing, coupled with the writer's insistence on a play embodying an idea, make it a work of some interest.

Goldschmidt's next dramatic work to be staged was the two-act Aristophanic comedy *I den anden Verden* (*In the Other World*), which had its first performance on 13 January 1869. The plot, possibly suggested by a Ludvig Holberg comedy, *Jeppe paa Bierget* (*Jeppe of the Hill*), is that the leading character believes he has died and is in "the other world," and is now free to tell the truth concerning everything. This offers the opportunity for wide-ranging social satire—an opportunity of which, unfortunately, Goldschmidt did not take full advantage. His comic character, the weakling Didriksen, has let himself be so cowed by his superior that he has agreed to the marriage of his daughter with his superior's son, although the girl loves another. When he learns of his daughter's feelings, Didriksen has a seizure, and when he calls for his medicine, he is accidentally given the wrong mixture, and loses consciousness. When he comes to, he believes he has died. The doctor advises that he be humored until he recovers, and all those around him pretend to be in the other world, too. In this state, Didriksen is not afraid of telling his superior the truth, and the marriage is called off. Didriksen falls asleep finally and the doctor says he will be back to normal when he awakens.

As in the previous work, there is practically no action or real plot in *In the Other World*, but the dialogue is funny and the characterizations are finely drawn. Edgar Collin, however, called the work "rather . . . a pathological experiment in dialogue form than a real play."[4] It, too, had the advantage of an excellent cast of actors, and was performed seven times that season.

The last of Goldschmidt's dramatic works, the three-act *Rabbi'en og Ridderen* (*The Rabbi and the Knight* [1869]), was a notable achievement. As Edgar Collin described the production, it "fulfilled the demands that can be placed on a dramatic work designed for the stage. . . . Goldschmidt had not only found a superb subject matter, but also treated it in a method that was, in many respects, perfect."[5] The play was a reworking of the earlier *Rabbi Eliezer* (Goldschmidt had changed the title at the request of the theater, to honor the actor who was to play the part of Bertrand, the knight). Goldschmidt had drastically changed the ending. The play no longer ends with the father's curse taking full effect; it now ends with the dying rabbi revoking the power of the curse, with Isabella's refusal to abandon Bertrand, and with Bertrand's apparent acceptance back into the Christian society. The softening of Eliezer's curse is a theatrical improvement, but a philosophical weakening.

The Rabbi and the Knight was performed eight times; the premiere took place on 31 March 1869. The reaction of the audience was favorable; the accompanying music, composed by Henrik Rung (1807–1871), with old Jewish melodies as a basis, greatly contributed to the appreciative reception. The critics were almost unanimous in their praise of the play; there was only one dissenting voice—that of the young Georg Brandes, at that time the theater critic for the weekly *Illustreret Tidende*. His review, based perhaps less on objective critical principles than personal antipathies, does not by any means constitute a high point of his criticism. *The Rabbi and the Knight* also involved Goldschmidt in an irksome lawsuit with his former publisher (see p. 55 above).

None of Goldschmidt's dramatic works merits the lack of attention which has been their fate; certainly *The Rabbi and the Knight* should be assigned its place among those of Goldschmidt's works which not only represent his best artistic achievements, but also reveal the most of his personal intellectual development. The dramatic works were an attempt at embodying Goldschmidt's concrete dramatic principles—realism as opposed to sentimentalism, and ideational content rather than visual spectacle. His stage works are strongest in dialogue and character delineation, weakest in plot and action. Although they constitute a small part of Goldschmidt's total literary output, the plays represent the work of the mature writer and cannot be overlooked if a complete picture of his development and a thorough understanding of his importance to Danish literature are to be attained.

CHAPTER 5

Goldschmidt and World Literature

GOLDSCHMIDT was unquestionably the leading Danish prose writer of the 1860s, but he had to make way in the 1870s for the new wave in Danish literature, the so-called "Modern Breakthrough" of realism, for which he had prepared the way. He is probably at present best known in Denmark as the author of *A Jew*, while outside Denmark his name is unfortunately most frequently associated with his feud with Søren Kierkegaard, his part in which is still widely misunderstood and misinterpreted. His contemporaries could not agree on a literary label to affix to Goldschmidt; Brandes, the leader of the "Breakthrough," stamped him as a Romantic, while others called him a Realist. As Mogens Brøndsted has pointed out, he was neither[1]—or perhaps he was both.

I Foreign Influences

The Danish scholar Knud Wentzel has ably analyzed the foreign influences apparent in Goldschmidt's works.[2] As he observes, the other notable Danish writers of the time tended to look to German Romanticism for inspiration, while the mature Goldschmidt turned to the great English and French writers, especially Dickens and Balzac. Wentzel also points out that Goldschmidt was the first Danish writer to become interested in Stendhal, and that Goldschmidt's clear and precise style seems to be generally indebted to French literary prose. In his *Corsaren* period, Voltaire and Mérimée had been the sources of inspiration for Goldschmidt's wit and Romantic irony. And while most Danish writers of this period were preoccupied with Byron, Goldschmidt had been inspired by Goethe's Werther figure. Goethe's *Wilhelm Meister* probably affected the composition of *A Jew* and *Homeless*. During the *Homeless* period, Gold-

125

schmidt was occupied with his burgeoning Nemesis idea, the origins of which Wentzel sees in Plato and the Greek tragedians. Later, the Greek concept was to merge with a similar one from Jewish tradition. During Goldschmidt's last period, which extended from the early 1860s to his death and thus included his most productive decade, he received inspiration primarily from Dickens and Balzac, especially in the composition of *The Heir* and *The Raven*, and from Stendhal in matters of style.

Most critics agree that the style of the Old Norse sagas (Goldschmidt read them in Danish translation) was one of the probable sources of Goldschmidt's clear, concise handling of the language. The Danish critic Paul V. Rubow (1896–1972) is an exception—he calls the theory that the sagas had any effect on Goldschmidt's style a "fable."[3] As Wentzel notes, Goldschmidt was simply susceptible to the literary currents that were at the time affecting European writers in general. Goldschmidt, however, was unique in seeking inspiration in Jewish culture and tradition; he was the first Jewish writer in Denmark to attempt the serious study of the history of Jewish culture for the purpose of utilizing it in his work.

II *Goldschmidt's English Writings*

Goldschmidt's literary activity in English—not to be confused with English translations of his works made by others—has usually not been taken into account in assessing his significance as a writer. Although they comprise only a small part of his production, his English compositions are varied. Apart from their literary worth—and they are not insignificant—the fact that Goldschmidt was able to produce works in English adds to his importance to Danish and world literature. His English writings parallel his Danish works in genre; they include the novel, the short story, the Jewish legend, the fairy tale, the travel sketch, and the journalistic article. Most of his English writings, though based on his Danish originals, are not translations but reworkings. Some were so radically altered that they are almost unrecognizable, and it seems justifiable to consider them as separate works.

The novel is represented by the English version of *Homeless*, since it now seems to be clear that *Homeless, or a Poet's Inner Life* is essentially Goldschmidt's own work, edited, as were all his English writings, by Hester Rothschild. The English novel which Goldschmidt worked on for some time, the notes for which are preserved in the Royal Library, Copenhagen, also gives proof of his ability to produce more lengthy works in English. Goldschmidt's English short stories include "My Uncle and his House: A Story of Danish Life," which was printed in *Macmillan's Magazine* in 1863; "The Last Lucifer Match," "The Photographs and Mephistopheles," and "At St. Onofrio—Tasso's Life," all included in "The Society of Virtue at Rome," published serially in *The Victoria Magazine* in 1868 (the dates of publication of some of his stories in English journals can be misleading; Goldschmidt probably submitted almost all of his English writings for publication by the end of 1863). The collection of stories, with the same title, *The Society of Virtue at Rome*, was published as a book in 1868.

The Jewish legends and stories form a much greater proportion of Goldschmidt's English works than of his works in Danish; some were never published in Danish. His English stories with Jewish themes include "Aaron and Esther, or, Three Days of Rabbi Nathan Clausener's Life" in *Chambers's Journal* in 1863, "Rabbi Raschi: A Jewish Legend" in *Once a Week* in 1869, "Rabbi Akiba" in the collection "The Society of Virtue at Rome" in *The Victoria Magazine* in 1868, and the collection "Hebrew Legends in Two Parts" in *Chambers's Journal* in 1862. These Hebrew legends include "Rabbi Meir's Wife," "Alexander and the Skull," "Rabbi Joschuah and the Princess," "A Greek Philosopher and a Rabbi," ["Rabbi Jochanni"], "Rabbi Raschi" (not the same version as that in *Once a Week*), "The Kamzan," "The Bird that Sang to a Bridegroom" (later used in a Danish version in *Love Stories from many Lands*), "David's Death," "The Witnesses" (reprinted in *The Jewish Chronicle and Hebrew Observer* the same year; the Danish version appeared in "Ghetto" in 1865), "The Drunkard and his Sons," "Our Pledges," "The Ram," "Isaac," "Ambition," "Reward—Chastity," "The Wandering Jew," "Tolerance," "Solidarity of Sin," and "Martyrs."

The fairy tale was represented by "The Elf's Ring" (a complete reworking of "Don Cleophas"), which was published

128 MEÏR GOLDSCHMIDT

serially in *The Victoria Magazine* in 1864; and "A Tale of the
Huldra" (The Danish original of which had appeared in *Nord
og Syd* in 1849), which was included in "The Society of Virtue
at Rome" in *The Victoria Magazine* in 1868. "On the Danube,
and Among the Mountains," in *Chambers's Journal* in 1862 (a
reworking of material that had been printed in *Nord og Syd*
in 1856) was an example of Goldschmidt's travel sketch, and
examples of his journalistic writing are "A Norwegian Musician"
in *The Cornhill Magazine* in 1862, "Discoveries near Rome" in
The Athenæum in 1863, and a continuing commentary, "Social
Aspects of the Danish War," which ran in *The Athenæum* from
May through July 1864. Goldschmidt was also an occasional
writer of "letters to the editor"; his letters were printed in *The
Times, The Athenæum,* and *The Jewish Chronicle and Hebrew
Observer.*

The notes for the unfinished English novel, which was to
correct the "mistake" in *Homeless* where the hero is not a Jew,
are of considerable literary interest; in addition to the half-
concealed autobiographical material contained in them, and
the additional proof they afford of Goldschmidt's ability to
compose in English, they indicate that a work of some power
might have been produced if Goldschmidt had finished the
novel. The more or less complete outline of the first few
chapters, and the extensive additional scattered notes reveal
the following plot nucleus: The hero, a young descendant of
Sephardic Jews from Spain (see Alfons Mendoza in *Homeless*),
Manuel Rodrigues (the hero's name is later given as "Leon
Rodriguez"), meets the rich English Jew Marcus Melchior (evidently modeled on Benjamin Rothschild) and his family on
the Isle of Wight, and turns out to be Melchior's nephew. The
Melchiors have a fifteen-year-old daughter, Ellen, with whom
the hero soon falls in love. Leon is a gifted poet and musician,
and is described by Ellen's mother as a genius. (It is perhaps
significant that Goldschmidt, in describing his hero in a note
to Hester Rothschild—preserved among his papers in the Royal
Library—insists that he is not attempting a self-portrait.) The
young man comes to London to live with the Melchiors, and
comes into violent conflict with representatives of the orthodox
Jewish community there. His chief adversary is "Aaron White"

(Rabbi Aaron Green was one of Goldschmidt's antagonists in London); the names of two other of the young man's opponents —Franklin and Dr. Benish (Benisch)—are the real names of prominent and influential Jewish figures with whom Goldschmidt had difficulties. Much of the draft material for the novel is devoted to lengthy discussions concerning Judaism, apparently between the novel's hero and "Aaron White." These discussions probably are "transcripts" of actual conversations which took place between Goldschmidt and his orthodox opponents. In addition to the discussions of Judaism versus Christianity, there are notes indicating conversations concerning aesthetics. In one of these, which treats of the hero's understanding of the "ideal," he is asked, ". . . but of what practical use is it to hold forth an ideal, which we can never reach?" His (and Goldschmidt's) answer is, logically, "If we could reach it, it would be no ideal."

The material for this English "Jewish tale," as Goldschmidt called it, indicates that the novel, while evidently paralleling *Homeless* in general, might have been a more mature and more unified work, with the philosophical confrontation between Judaism and Christianity taking precedence over the problems of aesthetics. The "Jewish tale" would undoubtedly also have cast a much-needed light on some obscure corners of Goldschmidt's life in London in the early 1860s.

III *Goldschmidt's Legacy*

As Georg Brandes wrote, Goldschmidt's best legacy was his language—modern Danish literary prose.[4] Although apparently no later Danish writer has acknowledged a conscious indebtedness to Goldschmidt,[5] and one who is generally thought to have been influenced by Goldschmidt's style—the Nobel prize winner Henrik Pontoppidan (1857–1943)—has expressly denied being influenced,[6] the stylistic force of Goldschmidt's refined use of language has perhaps been much more pervasive than Goldschmidt's successors have been willing to acknowledge. His characteristic understatement and indirect expression (which irritated Georg Brandes), his typical treatment of his characters with simultaneous sympathy and gentle irony, and his combination of "fantasy" and "reality" are such subtle traits that it would be difficult to document their impact upon later writers.

A recent leading Danish prose writer whose work is often associated with that of Goldschmidt is the bilingual Karen Blixen ("Isak Dinesen"). Although she apparently never publicly expressed any debt to Goldschmidt, her use of language, as well as her views on Nemesis, is generally thought to stand in a certain indebtedness to Goldschmidt.[7]

A survey of the reprintings of Goldschmidt's works since his death shows that he has been read continually; while there have been periods during which none of his works were reprinted, the recurrent cycle of reprintings is constant and continues to the present. Although some of his Jewish stories are among his most popular works, it seems clear that Goldschmidt's fame has achieved the synthesis of the Danish and the Jewish that was never attained in his life. To the modern Danish reader he is only incidentally—by virtue of his superb Jewish stories—thought of as Jewish; he is acclaimed as one of the greatest Danish national writers.

Notes and References

Preface

1. Pp. 278–79.
2. II (Copenhagen: Gyldendal, 1899), 461–68. Translation by the present writer.
3. (Copenhagen: Hagerup, 1919).

Chapter One

1. See Morten Borup, ed., *Breve fra og til Meïr Goldschmidt* (Copenhagen: Rosenkilde & Bagger, 1963), I, 37.
2. *Meïr Goldschmidt* (Copenhagen: Gyldendal, 1965), p. 69. All translations from Danish sources are by the present writer, unless otherwise stated.
3. "M. Goldschmidt," *Samlede Skrifter,* vol. 2 (Copenhagen: Gyldendal, 1899), 453.
4. Not, as Morten Borup says in *Meïr Goldschmidts breve til hans familie* (Copenhagen: Rosenkilde & Bagger, 1964), I, 46, his more famous brother Theodor. See Lothar Wickert, *Theodor Mommsen: Eine Biographie,* vol. 2 (Frankfurt: Klastermann, 1964), p. 185; and Julius Ziehen, *Tycho Mommsen, geboren 1819, gestorben 1900* (Leipzig, 1904), p. 106. In writing of people he met on his travels, Goldschmidt usually used only last names; this sometimes makes positive identification difficult.
5. *Meïr Goldschmidts breve til hans familie,* I, 163.
6. Morten Borup, ed., *Breve fra og til Holger Drachmann* (Copenhagen: Gyldendal, 1968), p. 49.
7. See Elias Bredsdorff, *H. C. Andersen og Charles Dickens: Et venskab og dets opløsning* (Copenhagen: Rosenkilde & Bagger, 1951), pp. 36–37.
8. Not George Townsend, as Borup says (*Meïr Goldschmidts breve til hans familie,* II, 214). Goldschmidt, true to his habit, wrote of Townshend using only the last name, and, moreover, he spelled it "Townsend," but his description makes it clear that his acquaintance was Chauncey Hare Townshend.
9. *Meïr Goldschmidts breve til hans familie,* II, 34.

10. *Meïr Goldschmidts breve til hans familie*, II, 69.
11. *Meïr Goldschmidts breve til hans familie*, II, 60.
12. Knud Wentzel, "Fremmed indflydelse på M. Goldschmidts forfatterskab," 1965, p. 2. (An unpublished award-winning paper at the University of Copenhagen.)
13. *Quarterly Review*, 123 (1867), 417–64.
14. The draft of the letter is printed in *Breve fra og til Meïr Goldschmidt*, II, 134–40.
15. *Den danske Skueplads*, VII (Copenhagen: Forlagsbureauet, 1876), 414–16.
16. *M. Goldschmidt* (Copenhagen: Hagerup, 1919), II, 167.
17. The letter is printed in *Breve fra og til Meïr Goldschmidt*, II, 192–93; the obituary is in *The Athenæum*, 27 August 1887, pp. 278–79. There are a few unimportant discrepancies between Gosse's quotation and the published version of the letter.
18. 1887, reprinted in Brandes' *Samlede Skrifter*, II (Copenhagen: Gyldendal, 1899), 461–68.
19. Reprinted in *Samlede Skrifter*, II, 447–58.
20. *Dansk litteraturhistorie* (Copenhagen: Politiken, 1971), II, 691–92.
21. *A History of Danish Literature*, 2nd ed. (New York: Kraus-Thomson, 1971), p. 167.
22. *Goldschmidts fortællekunst* (Copenhagen, Gyldendal, 1967).

Chapter Two

1. *Goldschmidts fortællekunst*, p. 24.
2. *Goldschmidts fortællekunst*, p. 15; *Meïr Goldschmidt* (Copenhagen: Gyldendal, 1965), p. 69.
3. Anja Nathan, "En kulturhistorisk efterprøvning af de jødiske skildringer i Goldschmidts fortællinger," thesis, University of Copenhagen, 1959.
4. See Elias Bredsdorff, *H. C. Andersen og England* (Copenhagen: Rosenkilde & Bagger, 1954), pp. 183–84.
5. Cited in Elias Bredsdorff, *Hans Christion Andersen: The Story of his Life and Work 1805–75* (London: Phaidon, 1975), p. 190.
6. See Bredsdorff, *Hans Christian Andersen: The Story of his Life and Work 1805–75*, p. 214. For a full discussion of the incompetence of both ladies as translators, with examples of their ignorance of Danish, see Elias Bredsdorff, *H. C. Andersen og England*, pp. 489–94 and pp. 506–508.
7. *Livs Erindringer og Resultater* (Copenhagen: Rosenkilde & Bagger, 1965), I, 199.

8. See *Goldschmidts fortællekunst*, p. 19.

9. *Meïr Goldschmidts breve til hans familie*, II, 60.

10. *Nord og Syd*, n.s., vol. 4 (1853), 179.

11. *The Heir* (Bayswater: William Brunker, 1865). This listing apparently misled Morten Borup; see his edition of *Meïr Goldschmidts breve til hans familie*, I, 106.

12. Mogens Brøndsted identifies this motif as stemming from a Faroese folk tale (*Meïr Goldschmidt*, p. 170; *Goldschmidts fortællekunst*, p. 261) and cites as Goldschmidt's source *Antiquarisk Tidsskrift*, published in Copenhagen by Det kongelige Nordiske Oldskrift-Selskab, the volume for 1849–1851 (published 1852), p. 205. But the folk tale in question, "Sigursteinur," no. 14 of the "Færöiske Folkesagn, optegnede af V. U. Hammershaimb," differs in several significant details from that given by Goldschmidt.

Chapter Three

1. *Meïr Goldschmidts breve til hans familie*, II, 34.

2. Letter dated 6 May 1863, in *Meïr Goldschmidts breve til hans familie*, II, 87.

3. *The Victoria Magazine*, January 1868, p. 221.

4. Letter dated 13 September 1861, in *Meïr Goldschmidts breve til hans familie*, I, 240.

5. Letter dated 4 March 1863, in *Meïr Goldschmidts breve til hans familie*, II, 65.

6. Letter dated 3 May 1864, preserved among Goldschmidt's papers in the Royal Library, Copenhagen (NkS 4252,4⁰).

7. *Livs Erindringer og Resultater*, ed. Morten Borup (Copenhagen: Rosenkilde & Bagger, 1965), I, 208.

8. *Livs Erindringer og Resultater*, I, 74.

9. *Livs Erindringer og Resultater*, I, 132–37.

Chapter Four

1. According to Morten Borup (*Breve fra og til Meïr Goldschmidt*, III, 78), it appeared in 1862, the date (1863) on the title page notwithstanding.

2. *M. Goldschmidt*, II, 152.

3. In his continuation of Thomas Overskou's *Den danske Skueplads*, vol. 7 (Copenhagen: Forlagsbureauet, 1876), 413–14.

4. *Den danske Skueplads*, VII, 475.

5. *Den danske Skueplads*, VII, 477–78.

Chapter Five

1. *Goldschmidt's fortællekunst*, p. 256.
2. "Fremmed indflydelse på M. Goldschmidts forfatterskab," gold medal treatise at the University of Copenhagen (Alm. litteratur-videnskab, 1965).
3. See, for example, *Goldschmidt og Nemesis* (Copenhagen: Munksgaard, 1968), p. 5.
4. "M. Goldschmidt," *Samlede Skrifter*, vol. 2 (Copenhagen: Gyldendal, 1899), 468.
5. Among Goldschmidt's contemporaries, Vilhelm Bergsøe (1835–1911) produced works strongly reminiscent of Goldschmidt. Bergsøe's *Fra Piazza del Popolo* (1867) and *Fra den gamle Fabrik* (1869) were probably inspired by Goldschmidt's works.
6. Interview in *Politiken*, 19 December 1905, reprinted in Knut Ahnlund, ed., *Omkring Lykke-Per* (Copenhagen: Hans Reitzel, 1971), p. 61.
7. See, for example, Jørgen Gustava Brandt, "Ved Karen Blixens død," *Karen Blixen*, ed. Clara Svendsen and Ole Wivel (Copenhagen: Gyldendal, 1962), pp. 48–49; partially reprinted in Jørgen Gustava Brandt, ed., *Meïr Goldschmidt, digteren og journalisten: En mosaik af tekster* (Copenhagen: Danmarks Radio, 1974), pp. 108–10.

Selected Bibliography

PRIMARY WORKS

1. Danish Editions

Meïr Goldschmidt i Folkeudgave. 8 vols. Edited by Julius Salomon. Copenhagen: Gyldendal, 1908–1910. The "standard" selected works. Salomon's six-volume edition, *Udvalgte Skrifter,* published simultaneously, omits the two-volume *Hjemløs.*

Poetiske Skrifter. 8 vols. Edited by A. Goldschmidt. Copenhagen: Gyldendal, 1896–1898.

Breve fra og til Meïr Goldschmidt. 3 vols. Edited by Morten Borup. Copenhagen: Rosenkilde & Bagger, 1963.

Meïr Goldschmidts breve til hans familie. 2 vols. Edited by Morten Borup. Copenhagen: Rosenkilde & Bagger, 1964.

En Jøde: Novelle af Adolph Meyer. Copenhagen: "udgiven og forlagt af M. Goldschmidt," 1845.

Fortællinger. Af Adolph Meyer. Copenhagen: Reitzel, 1846.

Hjemløs. Copenhagen: Høst, 1853–1857. Published apparently simultaneously in *Nord og Syd.*

Blandede Skrifter. 4 vols. in 3. Copenhagen: Wroblewsky, 1859–1860.

Rabbi Eliezer: Dramatisk Digtning. Copenhagen: Wroblewsky, 1861.

Svedenborgs Ungdom: Dramatiseret Skildring. Copenhagen: Høst, 1863.

Fortællinger og Skildringer. 3 vols. Copenhagen: Steen, 1863–1865. Volume 3 contains *Arvingen.*

Dagbog fra en Reise paa Vestkysten af Vendsyssel og Thy. Copenhagen: Forlagsbureau, 1865.

Breve fra Choleratiden, indeholdende en lille Begivenhed. Copenhagen: Steen, 1865.

Arvingen. 2nd ed. Copenhagen: Steen, 1866.

En Hedereise i Viborg-Egnen. Copenhagen: Steen, 1867.

Kjærlighedshistorier fra mange Lande. Copenhagen: Steen, 1867.

Ravnen. Copenhagen: Steen, 1867.

En Roman i Breve. Copenhagen: Steen, 1867. Second edition of *Breve fra Choleratiden.*

135

En Skavank: Skuespil i tre Acter og med et Forspil. Copenhagen: Steen, 1867.
Den Vægelsindede paa Graahede. Copenhagen: Steen, 1867.
Smaa Fortællinger. Copenhagen: Steen, 1868–1869.
Rabbi'en og Ridderen: Drama i tre Acter. Copenhagen: Steen, 1869.
I den anden Verden: Komedie i to Acter. Copenhagen: Steen, 1869.
Avrohmche Nattergal. Copenhagen: Steen, 1871.
Fortællinger og Virkelighedsbilleder, ældre og nye. 2 vols. Copenhagen: Gyldendal, 1877.
Livs Erindringer og Resultater. 2 vols. Copenhagen: Gyldendal, 1877. Volume 2 contains "Nemesis." A fully annotated and indexed edition has been prepared by Morten Borup. Copenhagen: Rosenkilde & Bagger, 1965.
Fortællinger og Virkelighedsbilleder: Ny Samling. Copenhagen: Gyldendal, 1883.
Smaa Skildringer fra Fantasi og fra Virkelighed. Copenhagen: Gyldendal, 1887.

2. English Writings edited by Hester Rothschild

Homeless, or a Poet's Inner Life. 3 vols. London: Hurst and Blackett, 1861.
"A Norwegian Musician." *The Cornhill Magazine* 6 (1862), 514–27.
"On the Danube, and Among the Mountains." *Chambers's Journal,* 2 August 1862, pp. 65–70. Translation and reworking of "Fra en Reise: II. Paa Donau; III. Traunkirchen," published in *Nord og Syd, 1ste Qvartal* (1856), pp. 161–77; and "Mellem Bjergene," in *Nord og Syd, 3die Qvartal* (1856), pp. 213–22.
"Hebrew Legends: In Two Parts." *Chambers's Journal,* 4 October 1862, pp. 212–16; 11 October 1862, pp. 232–37. The first part contains "Rabbi Meir's Wife," "Alexander and the Skull," "Rabbi Joschuah and the Princess," "A Greek Philosopher and a Rabbi," ["Rabbi Jochanni"], and "Rabbi Raschi." Most had appeared in Danish in *Nord og Syd* in 1852; all (plus two additional legends) were printed in *Blandede Skrifter,* IV, 51–72. The second part contains "The Kamzan," "The Bird that Sang to a Bridegroom" (the Danish version of which appeared in *Kjærlighedshistorier fra mange Lande* [1867]), "David's Death," "The Witnesses" (reprinted in *The Jewish Chronicle and Hebrew Observer,* 17 October 1862, p. 7; the Danish version was included in "Ghetto" [1865]), "The Drunkard and his Sons," "Our Pledges," "The Ram," "Isaac," "Ambition," "Reward—Chastity," "The Wandering Jew," "Tolerance," "Solidarity of Sin," and "Martyrs."

"Aaron and Esther, or, Three Days of Rabbi Nathan Clausener's Life." *Chambers's Journal*, 24 January 1863, pp. 53–61. Translation and reworking of "Aron og Esther," *Fortællinger* (1846).

"Discoveries near Rome." *The Athenæum*, 13 June 1863, p. 779.

"My Uncle and his House: A Story of Danish Life." *Macmillan's Magazine* 7 (1863), 461–76. Translation and reworking of "Erindringer fra min Onkels Hus," *Fortællinger* (1846).

"Social Aspects of the Danish War," *The Athenæum*, 14 May 1864, pp. 676–77; 28 May 1864, pp. 741–42; 11 June 1864, pp. 806–807; 9 July 1864, pp. 51–52; 16 July 1864, pp. 82–83; 23 July 1864, pp. 116–17.

"The Elf's Ring." *The Victoria Magazine*, October 1864, pp. 508–31; November 1864, pp. 26–44; December 1864, pp. 129–37. A radical reworking of "Don Cleophas," which first appeared in *Nord og Syd* in 1856 and 1859, and was reprinted in *Blandede Skrifter*, I, 148–212; IV, 180–207.

"The Society of Virtue at Rome: Social Sketches." *The Victoria Magazine*, January 1868, pp. 216–31; February 1868, pp. 320–38; March 1868, pp. 399–422. Includes introduction, preprinted in *Once a Week* 15 (1866), 548–50; "The Last Lucifer Match," "The Photographs and Mephistopheles," "At St. Onofrio—Tasso's Life" (the Danish versions of all three of which appeared in *Fortællinger og Skildringer*, I, 49–193); "A Tale of the Huldra" (a reworking of material printed in *Nord og Syd* in 1849); and "Rabbi Akiba" (never published in Danish). *The Society of Virtue at Rome* was reprinted from *The Victoria Magazine* and published separately by Emily Faithfull's Victoria Press, 1868.

"Rabbi Raschi: A Jewish Legend." *Once a Week* 20 (1869), 346–49. Not the same version as that published in *Chambers's Journal*.

3. English Translations

En Jøde: (1) *Jacob Bendixen, the Jew*. Adapted from the Danish by Mary Howitt. 3 vols. London: Colburn & Co., 1852. Reprinted in 1 vol., London: Chapman & Hall, 1864. (2) *The Jew of Denmark: A Tale*. Translated by Mrs. [Anne S.] Bushby. London: George Routledge & Co., 1852. Also issued as No. 41 in Routledge's Railway Library.

"Assar og Mirjam": "Assar and Mirjam ('Love Stories from Many Countries')." Translated by Olga Flinch. Library of the World's Best Literature, Ancient and Modern, Memorial Edition in

Forty-Six Volumes, edited by Charles Dudley Warner, vol. 16, pp. 6495–500. New York: J. A. Hill & Co., 1896. Reprinted in Library of the World's Best Literature, Ancient and Modern, Special Edition in Thirty Volumes; vol. 11, pp. 6495–500. New York: The International Society, 1897.

"Avrohmche Nattergal": "Avrohmche Nightingale." Translated by Lida Siboni Hanson. In *Denmark's Best Stories: An Introduction to Danish Fiction;* Edited by Hanna Astrup Larsen; pp. 71–116. New York: Norton, 1928. Reprinted in *The Jewish Caravan: Great Stories of Twenty-Five Centuries;* pp. 458–77. Edited by Leo Walder Schwarz, New York: Rinehart, 1935. Reprinted in same book title, same pagination, Philadelphia: The Jewish Publication Society of America, 1946; and New York: Holt, Rinehart & Winston, [1965].

"Bjergtagen I": "Bewitched." Translated by Kenneth Ober. In *Anthology of Danish Literature;* Edited by F. J. Billeskov Jansen and P. M. Mitchell; pp. 242–61. Carbondale: Southern Illinois University Press; London: Feffer & Simons, 1971. Paperback edition, 1972.

"Den flyvende Post": (1) "The Flying Mail." Translated by Carl Larsen. In *The Flying Mail by M. Goldschmidt; Old Olaf by Magdalene Thoresen; The Railroad and the Churchyard by Björnstjerne Björnson;* pp. 7–42. Boston and Cambridge: Sever, Francis & Co., 1870. Reprinted in *Stories by Foreign Authors,* vol. 9; *Scandinavian,* pp. 39–81. New York: Charles Scribner's Sons, 1898. Reprinted 1899. Reprinted in Short Story Index Reprint Series, facsimile edition. Freeport, New York: Books for Libraries Press, 1970. (2) "The Wind as Post Office." In *A Stork's Nest, or, Pleasant Reading from the North;* edited by John Fulford Vicary; pp. 107ff. London and New York: F. Warne & Co., n.d.

"Henrik og Rosalie": "Henrik and Rosalie." Translated by Minna Wreschner. *American-Scandinavian Review* 10 (1922), 423–29. Reprinted in *Great Short Stories of the World,* edited by Barrett Harper Clark and Maxim Lieber, pp. 760–66. New York: Albert & Charles Boni, 1925. Reissued, Cleveland and New York: The World Publishing Co., and reprinted 1947 with same pagination. Reprinted in *World-Wide Short Stories,* edited by Roger B. Goodman. New York: Globe Book Co., 1966.

"Mendel Hertz": "Mendel Hertz." Translated by J. B. C. Watkins. In *A Golden Treasury of Jewish Literature;* edited by Leo W. Schwarz. pp. 150–56. New York and Toronto: Farrar & Rinehart, 1937.

"Paolo og Giovanna": "Paolo and Giovanna." Translated by Evelyn Heepe. *Lauritzen News* (Copenhagen), no. 17, (1951), pp. 15–16.

Note: The "translation" of *Arvingen* listed in the British Museum catalog as *The Heir*. Bayswater: William Brunker, 1865, is a seven-page brochure containing an excerpt from the first chapter, and the last chapter; probably translated by Goldschmidt himself.

SECONDARY WORKS

ANDERSEN, VILHELM. "Bjergtagen: Et motiv hos Goldschmidt." *Edda* 1 (1914), 75–87. Contributed greatly to popularizing and perpetuating the myth of Mrs. Stilling's all-pervasive influence on Goldschmidt's writings of the 1860s.
BONDEBJERG, IB. "Den hjemløse myte—en ideologikritisk analyse: Om dannelsesromanen og Goldschmidts Hjemløs." *Kritik* 23 (1972), 5–24. An "ideological-critical" analysis of the *Bildungsroman*, with application to *Hjemløs*.
BORUP, MORTEN. "Goldschmidtiana." *Danske Studier* 61 (1966), 106–18. Three articles: on discussion of the writer by Joseph Michaelsen (Goldschmidt's cousin) in his memoirs; on a youthful short story of Goldschmidt's, published under a pseudonym; and a half-concealed caricature of Goldschmidt in an Ingemann story.
BRANDES, GEORG. "M. Goldschmidt." *Samlede Skrifter*. Vol. 2. Copenhagen: Gyldendal, 1899, 447–68. Three articles, first published at different times; judgment affected by personal feelings and mutual lack of understanding.
BRANDT, JØRGEN GUSTAVA, ed. *Meïr Goldschmidt, digteren og journalisten: En mosaik af tekster*. [Copenhagen]: Danmarks Radio, 1974. A collection of extracts from Goldschmidt's works and from books and articles about Goldschmidt, illustrating his life and works.
BREDSDORFF, ELIAS. *Goldschmidts "Corsaren": Med en udførlig redegørelse for striden mellem Søren Kierkegaard og "Corsaren"*. [Aarhus]: Sirius, 1962. Carefully documented history of Goldschmidt's periodical and his feud with Kierkegaard.
BREDSDORFF, MORTEN. "Digteren Goldschmidt og Grundtvig: Et opgør om Nationalitet og Danskhed." *Grundtvig Studier* (1974), pp. 26–50. Traces and analyzes Grundtvig's attacks on Goldschmidt for being a "foreigner" and a "guest" in Denmark,

because he was a Jew, with no right to criticize or instruct the
Danish people.

BRØNDSTED, MOGENS. *Goldschmidts fortællekunst.* Copenhagen:
Gyldendal, 1967. Summarizes and analyzes Goldschmidt's major
works.

——————. *Meïr Goldschmidt.* Copenhagen: Gyldendal, 1967. Popular,
well-written biography; relies heavily on Hans Kyrre's work.

EGEBAK, JØRGEN. "Alting og forstanden: Meïr Goldschmidt,
Bjergtagen I-II." In *Analyser af dansk kortprosa,* vol. 1. Edited
by Jørgen Dines Johansen. Copenhagen: Borgen, 1971, 204–25.
Analyzes structures of the two "fairy tales" together.

KYRRE, HANS. *M. Goldschmidt.* 2 vols. Copenhagen: Hagerup, 1919.
Earliest complete biography of Goldschmidt; contains many
minor errors of fact and interpretation.

NATHAN, ANJA. "En kulturhistorisk efterprøvning af de jødiske
skildringer i Goldschmidts fortællinger." University of Copenhagen (Det filosofiske fakultet), 1959. A thesis assessing the
authenticity of Goldschmidt's descriptions of Jewish traditions,
rites, and customs.

OBER, KENNETH H. "Meïr Goldschmidt as a Writer of English."
Orbis Litterarum 29 (1974), 231–44. Discusses Goldschmidt's
writings during the period he was attempting to make a name
as a writer in England.

RUBOW, PAUL V. *Goldschmidt og Kierkegaard.* Copenhagen:
Gyldendal, 1952. Title is misleading; contains two unrelated
essays, one on each of the writers.

——————. *Goldschmidt og Nemesis.* Copenhagen: Munksgaard, 1968.
Along with useful information, contains much that is irrelevant.

SØHOLM, EJGIL. "Goldschmidts brevroman: Nogle bemærkninger
til værkets efterskrift." *Danske Studier* 67 (1972), 122–25.
Discusses the genesis of the "ideal" feminine portrait in *Breve
fra Choleratiden.*

——————. "Goldschmidts to jyske fortællinger." *Danske Studier* 63
(1968), 27–59. A thorough comparative analysis of *Den
Vægelsindede paa Graahede* and "Ekko'et."

TOLDBERG, HELGE. "Goldschmidt og Kierkegaard." In *Festskrift
til Paul V. Rubow,* pp. 211–35. Copenhagen: Gyldendal, 1956.
Traces Goldschmidt's relationship to Kierkegaard after 1846
on the basis of previously unpublished notes among Goldschmidt's papers in the Royal Library.

WENTZEL, KNUD. "Fremmed indflydelse på M. Goldschmidts forfatterskab." University of Copenhagen (Alm. litteraturviden-

skab), 1965. Thesis awarded the gold medal by the university; analyzes the foreign influences on Goldschmidt's works.

————. "Meïr Goldschmidt: *Arvingen.*" *Fortolkning og Skæbne: Otte danske romaner fra romantismen og naturalismen.* [Copenhagen]: Fremad, 1970, pp. 13–38. Discussion of the role of fate and the hero's quest for the key to its interpretation in the novel.

————. "Udvikling og påvirkning: Goldschmidts vej fra korsar til skriftklog." *Kritik* 10 (1969), 52–89. Traces the connections and dividing lines among the three phases of Goldschmidt's development; builds on the author's gold medal work on foreign influences.

Index

All the Year Round, 105

Andersen, Hans Christian, 25, 40, 44, 70, 71

Arena, 24, 25

Arentzen, Kristian, 49

Asbjørnsen, Peter Christen, 35, 36

Athenæum, The, 41, 57, 92, 128

Auerbach, Berthold, 43

Baggesen, Jens, 25

Balzac, Honoré de, 125, 126

Bauernfeldt, Eduard von, 31

Benisch, Dr. Abraham, 41, 49, 129

Bentley, Richard, 70, 71

Bergsøe, Vilhelm, 49, 50

Bjørnson, Bjørnstjerne, 36, 54, 106

Blicher, Steen Steensen, 27, 53, 109, 115

Blixen, Karen, 60, 130

Blixen Finecke, C. F., 37, 38

Blum, Robert, 31

Borgen, Vilhelm, 19, 20

Brandes, Georg, 27, 55, 58, 59, 84, 124, 125, 129

Bredsdorff, Elias, 28, 30, 40

Bretteville, Lodovica de, 38, 42

Brøndsted, Mogens, 27, 59, 62, 71, 93, 125

Brownhill, Thomas Robson, 47

Bull, Ole, 36, 47

Bushby, Mrs. Anne, 41, 70, 71

Byron, George Gordon, 125

Castelli, Ignaz von, 31

Chambers, Robert, 45, 48, 100

Chambers's Journal, 45, 47, 48, 100, 102, 106, 127, 128

Chievitz, Poul, 23

Christian VIII, 22, 34

Collin, Edgar, 55, 122, 123

Cornhill Magazine, The, 36, 45, 47, 128

Corsaire-Satan, Le, 23

Deutsch, Immanuel, 53

Dickens, Charles, 40, 42, 105, 125, 126

Dietrichson, Lorentz, 49, 50

Dietrichson, Mathilde, 49

"Dinesen, Isak." *See* Blixen, Karen

Disraeli, Benjamin, 40, 42

Drachmann, Holger, 39

Dreier, Frederik, 40, 41, 58

Edwards, Henry Sutherland, 46, 47

Fædrelandet (The Fatherland), 28, 29, 30, 45

Faithfull, Emily, 45, 103

Fibiger, Mathilde, 38, 42

Fischer, Kuno, 51

Frankl, Ludwig A., 31

Franklin, Jacob Abraham, 49, 129

Frederik VI, 22

Frederik VII, 34

Gade, Niels, 31

Gæa, 24, 29, 99

Goethe, Johann Wolfgang von, 125

Goldschmidt, Adolf, 25, 58, 113

Goldschmidt, Aron, 18, 19, 20, 21, 22

Goldschmidt, Lea (Meïr's mother), 18, 20, 55, 64

Goldschmidt, Meïr (Meyer), and anti-Semitism, 19, 26, 56, 61; and censorship, 21, 22, 23, 25, 30, 34; "Nemesis," 19, 26, 52, 56, 57, 58, 61, 73, 78, 79, 81, 82, 83, 84, 86, 87, 88, 89, 91, 92, 93, 94, 97,

100, 103, 107, 108, 109, 110, 111, 112, 114, 115, 116, 118, 119, 120, 121, 122, 126, 130

JOURNALISM:

Corsaren (The Corsair), 23, 24, 25, 28, 29, 30, 31, 34, 35, 42, 44, 54, 70, 119, 125
Hjemme og Ude (At Home and Abroad), 44
Nestved Ugeblad (Næstved Weekly), 21, 22, 58, 113
Norg og Syd (North and South), 34, 35, 36, 37, 38, 39, 41, 42, 43, 47, 54, 72, 85, 100, 101, 105, 119, 128

WORKS: NOVELS:

Arvingen (The Heir), 43, 52, 61, 86-92, 97, 102, 126
Hjemløs (Homeless), 24, 32, 40, 42, 43, 51, 61, 72-86, 87, 89, 92, 93, 97, 114, 125, 126, 128, 129
En Jøde (A Jew), 18, 20, 26, 27, 28, 30, 37, 41, 43, 61-72, 73, 85, 93, 97, 125
Ravnen (The Raven), 53, 57, 61, 93-97, 108, 109, 112, 126

WORKS: COLLECTIONS OF STORIES:

Blandede Skrifter (Mixed Writings), 98, 100, 102
Fortællinger (Stories), 30, 48, 98
Fortællinger og Skildringer (Stories and Descriptions), 52, 86, 98, 102, 103, 105
Fortællinger og Virkelighedsbilleder, ældre og nye (Stories and Pictures of Reality, older and new), 58, 98, 110
Fortællinger og Virkelighedsbilleder, Ny Samling (Stories and Pictures of Reality, New Collection), 58, 98, 111
Kjærlighedshistorier fra mange Lande (Love Stories from many Lands), 47, 52, 98, 102, 106, 108, 127

Smaa Fortællinger (Little Stories), 52, 98, 108, 110
Smaa Skildringer fra Fantasi og fra Virkelighed (Little Descriptions from Fantasy and from Reality), 58, 98, 112, 113

WORKS: STORIES (only the more representative of the individual stories are listed here):
"Aron og Esther" ("Aron and Esther"), 48, 99, 100
Avrohmche Nattergal, 54, 98, 115-16
"Bjergtagen I" ("Bewitched [No. 1]"), 52, 108, 109-10
Breve fra Choleratiden (Letters from the Cholera Time), 53, 98, 113-14
"Don Cleophas," 100, 101, 103, 127
"Erindringer fra min Onkels Hus" ("Memories from my Uncle's House"), 99
"Gift" ("Poison"), 110-11
Jewish legends, 101
"En Jul paa Landet" ("A Christmas in the Country"), 102, 105
"Maser," 53, 108-109
"Paolo og Giovanna" ("Paolo and Giovanna"), 106-107
En Roman i Breve (A Novel in Letters). See Breve fra Choleratiden
"Slaget ved Marengo" (The Battle at Marengo"), 117
Den Vægelsindede paa Graahede (The Fickle Girl on Graahede), 53, 98, 114-15

WORKS: DRAMA:

I den anden Verden (In the Other World), 55, 122-23
Rabbi Eliezer, 46, 47, 54, 55, 119-21, 123
Rabbi'en og Ridderen (The Rabbi and the Knight), 47, 55, 123-24
En Skavank (A Flaw), 54, 122

Svedenborgs Ungdom (*Swedenborg's Youth*), 46, 54, 121-22
"Vagabonden" ("The Vagabond"),
54

WORKS: TRAVEL SKETCHES:

*Dagbog fra en Reise paa Vest-
kysten af Vendsyssel og Thy*
(*Journal of a Trip on the West
Coast of Vendsyssel and Thy*),
52, 53, 98, 99, 117, 118
En Hedereise i Viborg-Egnen (*A
Trip Through the Heath in the
Viborg District*), 53, 99, 117,
118

WORKS: AUTOBIOGRAPHY:

Livs Erindringer og Resultater
(*Life's Recollections and Results*), 110

WORKS: ENGLISH WRITINGS:

"Aaron and Esther," 48, 100, 127
"Elf's Ring, The," 101, 102, 127,
128
"Hebrew Legends," 47, 102, 127
Homeless, or a Poet's Inner Life,
43, 45, 73, 85, 86, 97, 126, 127
"My Uncle and his House," 99,
127
"On the Danube, and Among the
Mountains," 47, 128
"The Society of Virtue at Rome"
(collection of short stories),
127, 128
"Tale of the Huldra, A," 128

Goldschmidt, Moritz, 31, 94
Goldschmidt, Ragnhild, 18, 20, 55
Goldschmidt, Theodora, 25
Goldsmid, Sir Francis, 85
Goldsmid, Sir Isaac L., 41
Goose with the Golden Eggs, The
(Edwards and Mayhew), 47
Gosse, Sir Edmund, 57, 59
Green, Rabbi Aaron Levy, 41, 48,
49, 129
Grillparzer, Franz, 31

Grundtvig, N. F. S., 18, 25, 34
Gutzkow, Karl, 31

Hambro, Joseph, 70
Hauch, Carsten, 54, 55, 56
Hebbel, Friedrich, 31
Heiberg, Johan Ludvig, 54
Heine, Heinrich, 33, 37
Henriksen Fladager, Ole, 49
Hertz, Henrik, 18
Hertz, Martin, 33
Høst, A. F., 35
Holbech, Carl Frederik, 49
Holberg, Ludvig, 25, 27, 122
Hostrup, Jens, 35
Howitt, Mary, 41, 70, 71, 85
Hugo, Victor, 37

Jeppe paa Bierget (*Jeppe of the
Hill*, Holberg), 122
Jewish Chronicle, The, 41, 49, 102,
127, 128
Jews' College, London, 48
Josephson, Jacob A., 31

Kierkegaard, Søren, 27, 28, 29, 30,
125
Klæstrup, Peter, 29
Köberle, Georg, 31
Kompert, Leopold, 31
Kyrre, Hans, 56, 122

Laube, Heinrich, 43
Lesage, Alain René: *Le diable
boiteux*, 101
Levin, Heyman, 18
Levin, Martin, 39
Liunge, A. P., 20
Lytton, Edward Bulwer, 42

Macmillan's Magazine, 45, 99, 127
Masson, David, 45
Mayhew, Augustus Septimus, 46, 47
Mérimée, Prosper, 125
"Meyer, Adolph" (Goldschmidt),
26, 27, 30
Meyers, Barnett, 48, 49
Michaelsen, Joseph, 44

Mitchell, P. M., 59
Moe, Jørgen, 35, 36, 109
Møller, Peder Ludvig, 24, 25, 26, 28, 29, 43, 75, 99
Mommsen, Karl J. T., 33
Montefiore ,Sir Moses, 41, 81
Munch, Andreas, 32, 35
Munch, Charlotte, 32, 35, 36

Nathan, Anja, 63

Oehlenschläger, Adam, 24
Olrik, Henrik, 49
Once a Week, 127
Oscar I, 36
Overskou, Thomas, 55

Payable on Demand (Taylor), 46, 47
Pescantini, Federigo, 32
Petersen, Clemens, 53, 54
Ploug, Carl, 24, 77
Pontoppidan, Henrik, 129

"Raphael, Clara." *See* Fibiger, Mathilde
"Robson, Frederick." *See* Brownhill, Thomas Robson
Rohde, Peter P., 59
"Romana." *See* Bretteville, Lodovica de
Rosenberg, Carl, 43
Rosenkilde, Adolph, 35, 42
Rosenkilde, Anna, 35, 42, 43
Rosenkilde, Christen Niemann, 54, 119
Rothschild, Benjamin, 18, 32, 39, 40, 41, 43, 44, 48, 49, 52, 85, 128
Rothschild, Hester, 39, 40, 41, 45, 48, 49, 52, 85, 104, 105, 106, 127, 128
Rowan, Frederica Maclean, 41, 45, 85

Rubow, Paul V., 126
Ruge, Arnold, 31, 40
Rung, Henrik, 124

Saabye, August, 49
Saphir, Moritz, 31
Schmidt, Valdemar, 49
Schwartz, Maria Espérance von "Elpis Melena"), 50, 105, 106
Seidelin, Pauline, 26
"Sibylla." *See* Bretteville, Lodovica de
"Society of Virtue" ("Dydsforeningen"), 49, 50, 103, 104
Sonne, Johanne Marie, 25, 26, 35, 88, 113
Stendhal (Marie Henri Beyle), 125, 126
Stilling, Christiane Louise, 49, 50, 51, 52, 90, 105, 118
Stilling, Peter M., 49, 50, 51, 118

Talmud, 53
Taylor, Tom, 46
Times, The (London), 128
Townshend, Chauncey Hare, 42

Up at the Hills (Taylor), 46

Varnhagen von Ense, Karl A., 33, 37
Varnhagen von Ense, Rahel, 33
Victoria Magazine, The, 36, 102, 103, 127, 128
Vinje, Aasmund Olafsson, 36
Voltaire, 125

Wagner, Richard, 43
Welhaven, Johan Sebastian, 35, 36
Wentzel, Knud, 52, 125, 126
Wergeland, Henrik, 24
Wilkinson, J. J. G., 121
Winge, Mårten Eskil, 50